Revised Printing

*College, Career
and Beyond...*

A Toolkit For Success

NEW ENGLAND INSTITUTE OF TECHNOLOGY · 1940 ·

COLLEGE, CAREER AND BEYOND: A TOOLKIT FOR SUCCESS

Edited by
Sharon J. Charette
Learning Resources Center Director
New England Institute of Technology

KENDALL/HUNT PUBLISHING COMPANY
4050 Westmark Drive   Dubuque, Iowa 52002

The book cover was designed by Diane M. Wetzel, one of the College's first TEC 101 students, who is in the Internet Communications Technology program.

DEDICATION

This book is dedicated to Jeanne Sjovall, Special Assistant to the Provost for Institutional Advancement, whose energy was the guiding force behind the creation of this course and the completion of this book. For over twenty years, she has inspired students, faculty and staff with her enthusiasm, her wit and her overwhelming commitment to bringing out the hidden talents in all of us. Jeanne has been mentor, advisor, teacher and friend. As she retires and takes on the new role of part-time instructor, she will undoubtedly continue to motivate all of us who will forever remain indebted to her. Jeanne's dedication to the entire New England Tech community has taught us all to reach for the stars.

CONTENTS

Acknowledgments

Editorial Board

The editorial board edited the text, selected supporting articles and coordinated all of the details that went into the completion of the book.

Karen Arnold, Assistant Dean

Sharon J. Charette, Learning Resources Center Director

Stephanie A. Ferriola, Coordinator of Competency-Based Faculty Development

Catherine Kennedy, Vice President for Career Development

Ann M. Ricci, Assistant Professor of Administrative Medical Assistant Technology

Jeanne Sjovall, Special Assistant to the Provost for Institutional Advancement

TEC 101 Planning Committee

The following individuals were responsible for the design of the course.

Chair: Jeanne Sjovall, Special Assistant to the Provost for Institutional Advancement

Karen Arnold, Assistant Dean

Steve Berrien, Senior Vice President and Provost

Mary L. Branco, Coordinator for High School Program

Steven S. Calabro, Director of Counseling Services

Sharon J. Charette, Learning Resources Center Director

Mary Jean Clapp, Associate Professor of Computer and Network Servicing Technology

David J. Cranmer, Associate Professor of Humanities and Social Science

Kathy Duggan, Instructor of Computerized Business Management Technology

Catherine Kennedy, Vice President for Career Development

Doreen Lasiewski, Director of Instructional Development

Joyce Lawrence, Instructor of Mathematics

Margaret McKenna, Assistant Professor, Chair of Electrical Technology

Judith A. Nabb, Coordinator of Reading and Study Skills

Lee Peebles, Director of Student Advising

Ann M. Ricci, Assistant Professor of Administrative Medical Assistant Technology

Peter R. Schuyler, Associate Professor of Electronics Engineering Technology

F. Leon Sibielski, Instructor of Humanities and Social Science

Thomas P. Strolla, Assistant Professor of Video and Radio Production Technology

First Quarter Facilitators

After the course was designed, facilitators chosen from faculty and administration delivered the course to students. They have contributed significantly to its redesign by providing valuable feedback and evaluation.

John A. Cormier, Associate Professor, Chair of Video and Radio Production/ Telecommunications Technologies

Kathy Duggan, Instructor of Computerized Business Management Technology

Stephanie A. Ferriola, Coordinator of Competency-Based Faculty Development

John P. Gauthier, Chief Academic Advisor

Robert J. Goldberg, Instructor of Humanities and Social Science

Diane E. Johnson, Student Advisor

Michael Kwiatkowski, Director of Admissions

Mary Ann Neary, Student Advisor

Fran O'Connell, Skills Specialist, Academic Skills Center

Colette Recupero, Coordinator of Academic Services, Office of Teaching and Learning

Donald L. Soucy, Associate Professor of Humanities and Social Science

Geneva Urquhart, Instructor of Humanities and Social Science

Additional Contributors

The following staff members also contributed to the creation of this textbook:

Michelle Rotmer Duffy, Skills Specialist, Academic Skills Center

Louise Hamelin, Coordinator of Computer Services, Academic Skills Center

Joseph Holland, Reference Librarian

Cassandra J. Lovejoy, Reference Librarian

Susan C. McAllister, Skills Specialist, Academic Skills Center

Cynthia A. Pankiewicz, Catalog Librarian

Charles K. Rogers, Special Assistant to the President

Leslie E. Tracey, Technical Services Assistant, Learning Resources Center

INTRODUCTION

The TEC 101 First Quarter Professional Seminar and this book are the result of nearly two years of collaboration among the staff, faculty and students of New England Institute of Technology. The process began on July 14, 1998, when Jim Tully, Vice-President for Student Services; Jeanne Sjovall, Special Assistant to the Provost; and Dr. Steve Calabro, Director of Student Counseling, attended a regional two-day workshop hosted by John N. Gardner and Betsy O. Barefoot from the National Resource Center for The First-Year Experience & Students in Transition, University of South Carolina. The three returned to the campus convinced that a first-quarter course, similar to those being offered in many other colleges and universities, would greatly benefit our students. They brought their proposal to Provost Steve Berrien and to Seth Kurn, Executive Vice-President, and in a series of meetings over six months, worked out what such a course would involve and appointed a planning committee of content specialists from throughout New England Tech.

The planning committee designed the course that is now TEC 101. The course became a graduation requirement and was offered for the first time in the Winter Quarter 2000. Students and facilitators evaluated each module and recommended changes that would ensure that the course met the needs of beginning students. When TEC 101 ran in the Spring Quarter, there were significant revisions. Close attention had been paid to what NEIT students expect and believe is important to their academic, career and personal success.

College, Career and Beyond: A Toolkit for Success is the result of the work of the planning committee, the facilitators and our students. This book is designed not only as a text-book for TEC 101 but as a handbook that you will use well beyond the first quarter to manage your life, strengthen your skills and prepare for a successful career.

Sharon J. Charette
Editor

New England
Institute of
Technology

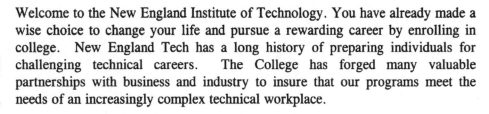

Dear Student:

Welcome to the New England Institute of Technology. You have already made a wise choice to change your life and pursue a rewarding career by enrolling in college. New England Tech has a long history of preparing individuals for challenging technical careers. The College has forged many valuable partnerships with business and industry to insure that our programs meet the needs of an increasingly complex technical workplace.

Part of the College's success lies in the campus-wide commitment to supporting our students with a wide range of resources designed to assist them in achieving their educational and career goals. TEC 101: The First Quarter Professional Seminar and this book will introduce you to many support services and resources available to students. TEC 101 was born out of the desire to equip students with the skills that they need to succeed in college and in life.

In the coming years, you will be challenged and inspired to become one of a growing number of successful graduates of New England Tech. The faculty and administration are confident that the skills that you learn here will prepare you to become productive members of the community. It is our sincere hope that you take advantage of all of the opportunities and assistance available to help you succeed.

Sincerely,

Richard I. Gouse
President

2500 Post Road
Warwick, RI
02886-2266
Tel: 401-467-7744
Fax: 401-738-5122
www.neit.edu
neit@neit.edu

CHAPTER 1
Beginning the Journey

"I entered NEIT with the goal of working in an operating room. I knew that with hard work, discipline and dedication, my goal would be met. The faculty are devoted to their students, and with their help, anyone can be "all that they can be." Because of their dedication and support, I was able to become an integral member of Rhode Island Hospital's operating room staff."

Mary Love
Surgical Technology

Chapter Designers:

Mary Jean Clapp, Associate Professor of Computer and Network Servicing Technology
Catherine Kennedy, Vice President for Career Development
Margaret McKenna, Assistant Professor, Chair of Electrical Technology
Ann M. Ricci, Assistant Professor of Administrative Medical Assistant Technology
Peter R. Schuyler, Associate Professor of Electronics Engineering Technology
Thomas P. Strolla, Assistant Professor of Video & Radio Production Technology

What Students Are Saying . . .

"During this course, I felt so happy about my decision to come to NEIT, not only because of the high esteem the institution is being held among other institutions in the country, but also because of its educational philosophy, i.e. to give equal opportunities to students from different educational backgrounds regardless of race, disabilities and religious, ethnic and gender disparity."

Adenigba Henry Aribisala
Electronics Technology

In This Chapter

■ You will get an orientation to New England Institute of Technology (NEIT)—its history, mission, organization—and to the academic curricula.

■ Introduction

For over sixty years, New England Institute of Technology (NEIT) has been a leader in technical education. By tailoring its curriculum to respond to the needs of business and industry, the College successfully educates individuals who can enter the workforce confident in their technical skills. NEIT's history illustrates a commitment to maintaining a student-centered environment able to meet the needs of students and employers.

This chapter provides an overview of the goals and objectives of this course as well as useful information about what is expected of you and what you should expect from your college experience. Your journey toward an exciting technical career begins here with the first step of learning about the College's past and what it means for your future.

■ The History of New England Institute of Technology: From Post World War II Into the New Millennium, by Charles K. Rogers, Special Assistant to the President

A Modest Beginning

Back in 1940, Mr. Ernest G. Earle, the founder of what was to become New England Institute of Technology, stretched out his hand fewer than 20 times to congratulate the first class to complete his course in radio repair. The school consisted of three rented rooms on the sixth floor of an office building in downtown Providence.

It's quite possible that the last thing on Mr. Earle's mind was the notion that in 60 years New England Institute of Technology would be a thriving college serving thousands of students from all around the country and the world. His goal was to provide practical, hands-on training at reasonable cost—training that would lead to a job that was a cut above the factory work that was the norm for the times. He was constantly watching the evolution of the economy and was not afraid to respond.

When soldiers came home from World War II, New England Institute of Technology had already invested in a laboratory to offer courses in plastics technology, an infant industry that was about to boom. In those early days, Mr. Earle's students were practical, serious-minded people. The first graduation ceremony lasted less than 15 minutes. It is said that some in the class—who were all men—had to leave early to go back to work. Mr. Earle rode the swings in the economy much this way through the '50s and '60s. He invested in new training laboratories to teach electronics when electronics was becoming an important industry. He did the same by offering training in appliance and small engine repair and other new disciplines. Along the way he prospered, lost, reinvested and survived.

Looking back, we now marvel at how Mr. Earle was able to keep things together as well and for as long as he did. At the same time, we see clearly even today the powerful, binding ties that link our days as a trade school to the success we now enjoy as a college.

By the late 1960s, baby-boomers were entering the workforce by the millions. College degrees were now considered a necessity. Space-age technology was making it very difficult to break into a good job solely because an individual had talented hands and could read a manual. By 1971 it was obvious that New England Institute of Technology had to change direction.

Transition from Trade School to Computer Age College

A revolution was started in 1971 when Richard I. Gouse became the College's President. As the first order of business, the narrow definition of a trade school was abandoned and new professional programs were developed to meet the changing needs of the modern workplace. Investments were made in new equipment without any assurances that there would be students to make use of them.

Would students be able to go beyond the how-to's of operating and maintaining equipment? Would they be able to or even want to learn the theory and the communications skills that were essential to perform in the high-technology work environment? That question has now been answered by tens of thousands of our graduates in their performance on the job. Their success has become legendary.

By the end of the '70s, New England Institute of Technology had become a degree-granting college. In the '80s bachelor's degrees were conferred for the first time. When it became clear in the early '80s that New England Institute of Technology had to either embrace the computer age or fall by the wayside, the decision to upgrade the curriculum was the first and most important of many changes to come. Slowly at first, and then in greater and greater numbers, students began to fill the seats in front of factory-fresh computers and in newly-built science, mathematics and humanities classrooms.

Students learned that the idea wasn't to turn New England Institute of Technology into a traditional liberal arts college. Our faculty still focused on giving them specialized training in technical fields that suited their talents and inclination to work with their hands.

> **C**ountless employers consider New England Institute of Technology a primary resource for their hiring needs.

Our students came to realize that their ability to achieve in liberal arts courses would probably mean the difference between a job with little future or a promising career. Once that message got through, the revolution was underway. Soon it became clear that these young people, many of whom had never tasted success in school before, blossomed in the new learning environment.

College to Career

To ensure that our curricula were preparing students for the workplace, technical advisory committees were created. Today, we continue to rely upon the input of our technical advisors who come to us from business and industry. They meet with the College's department chairs to review our curricula and offer guidance as to what should be taught based upon the trends in industry and needs of employers.

Our ties to industry extend beyond our technical advisors. Countless employers consider New England Institute of Technology a primary resource for their hiring needs and contact the College looking for graduates. The College's Career Services Office also contacts employers to identify employment opportunities. As a result, each year new graduates join thousands of New England Institute of Technology graduates in exciting and rewarding careers.

At the Beginning of a New Millennium

Today more than 2,500 men and women attend classes at New England Institute of Technology, pursuing two- and four-year degrees in 27 technical programs accredited by the New England Association of Schools and Colleges, Inc.

The campus that started in an older mill-style building in Providence, Rhode Island, now encompasses two locations and includes ten buildings on almost 15 acres of land with approximately 175,000 square feet of state-of-the-art classroom, laboratory, faculty and administration office space.

Each spring, over 5,000 parents and friends crowd into a joyous commencement exercise honoring the nearly 1,000 men and women who have earned degrees from New England Institute of Technology.

Today the College includes:

- The largest library in Rhode Island specializing in the technologies
- Computer workstations in almost every classroom
- Expanded laboratories for the study of computers, electronics, CAD, medical technologies, transportation technologies, the building trades and related business technologies, the Internet, multimedia and much more
- Parking facilities for students, a full-service bookstore, a student lounge, leisure areas and food services

The College's credentials continue to grow as can be seen below:

- The Electronics program has been selected by the Federal Aviation Administration as an approved collegiate training center.
- The Automotive and Auto Body programs are certified at the master level by the National Automotive Technicians Education Foundation (NATEF) and have been selected as a Sikkins and PPG training site.
- New England Institute of Technology is the only authorized AutoDesk Premier Training Center in Rhode Island and is the only college in Rhode Island authorized as a NOVELL Educational Academic Partner.
- New England Institute of Technology is authorized by Microsoft Corporation as a Microsoft Solution Provider and is a Microsoft Authorized Technical Education Center.
- The bachelor's degree program in Electronics Engineering Technology is accredited by the Technology Accreditation Commission of the Accreditation Board for Engineering and Technology (ABET).

■ There is a training alliance with CADD Edge Inc. providing authorized training in the use of SolidWorks.

■ New England Institute of Technology is a training provider for the American Boat and Yacht Council and the American Boat Builders and Repairers Association; and the College's Marine Technology Department has been selected as a Volvo-Penta Training Site.

■ New England Institute of Technology is a training provider for the Manufacturing Partnership for Rhode Island Work Force Development and the New England Fuel Institute.

■ The College's Surgical Technology program is accredited by the Commission on Accreditation of Allied Health Education Programs (CAAHEP).

■ The Occupational Therapy Assistant Technology Program is accredited by the Accreditation Council for Occupational Therapy Education (ACOTE) of the American Occupational Therapy Association (AOTA).

> **A**ll persons . . . should have access to career opportunity through a quality technical education.

Our Educational Philosophy

New England Institute of Technology is a private, non-profit, technical college whose mission is to provide specialized associate and bachelor degree programs for students from diverse educational backgrounds and with differing levels of ability. The College's mission evolved from the principle that all persons, regardless of age, gender, disability, socio-economic circumstances, religious, racial or ethnic background, should have access to career opportunity through a quality technical education. To achieve this purpose, NEIT is first and foremost an institution committed to teaching.

NEIT believes and affirms that every student can learn; it recognizes that different students may learn in different ways with differing levels of ability; and it recognizes the importance of creating a learning environment in each classroom and laboratory that both challenges and supports. The method of instruction consists of hands-on technical education with a theoretical background, combined with the development of analytical skills in general education subjects. This combination of technical and analytical skills, monitored through performance-based assessments, uniquely prepares students for long-range employment opportunities.

At New England Institute of Technology, students participate in real world programs that offer excellent employment opportunities. The 1997 report of the Rhode Island Economic Policy Council boldly stated that a "robust Rhode Island economy needs to be one that emphasizes technology-based products and processes and a highly skilled workforce." New England Institute of Technology is at the forefront of technical education and is well-positioned to educate the workforce of tomorrow. To accomplish this goal, the College is fortunate to have a talented and sensitive faculty that knows how to bring out the best in our students. In addition, the College has forged a multitude of industry/education partnerships which the Council has underscored as vital to the growth of the economy. As a result of all this, we enjoy an excellent relationship with the industrial community in New England.

As we celebrate over 60 years since our founding, it is a pleasure and a source of great pride to look back over the highlights that trace New England Institute of Technology's growth and development over the years. Looking back gives us a new appreciation for the importance of the contributions of literally thousands of dedicated individuals to the success we enjoy today. Looking back also makes the exciting challenges that we face as we enter the new century seem all the more achievable.

Statement of Mission and Objectives

The mission of New England Institute of Technology (NEIT) is to provide specialized associate and bachelor degree programs which prepare students for technical careers.

N ew England Institute of Technology is at the forefront of technical education and is well-positioned to educate the workforce of tomorrow.

Through the combination of technical courses and an integrated liberal arts core, the programs emphasize the relevance of continuous learning to personal and professional growth. Upon successful completion, graduates are prepared to enter the workforce or to continue their education. As an extension of the primary mission, NEIT offers the opportunity to pursue technical studies to satisfy personal interests.

As an institution primarily devoted to teaching and through its open admission policy, NEIT provides opportunities for students from diverse educational backgrounds and with varying levels of ability to study technical fields.

NEIT's objectives are to:

1. offer technical programs that meet the career-oriented needs of students and to assist each student in identifying and developing a career path of interest.

2. stress the relationship between theoretical knowledge and practical application.

3. provide a laboratory approach which prepares students for business and industry.

4. enable students to develop skills in writing, oral communication, and team building.

5. use innovative learning approaches to help each student realize his or her academic potential.

6. help students to develop skills in problem-solving and in thinking logically, flexibly, and critically.

7. foster the student's potential to contribute to and participate in a rapidly changing technological society.

8. provide a campus climate where students are encouraged to respect the value of all people and to deal with the social problems and responsibilities they face as members of society.

9. encourage students to develop pride in the quality of their work.

10. create an appreciation for both the importance and joy of learning.

■ The Purpose and Goals of TEC 101

In order to assist you in attaining your career and life goals, TEC 101 has been designed to give you the tools that you need to succeed in your classes. Throughout the next ten weeks you'll get a chance to learn new things and to practice many of the new skills you have learned in a laboratory setting. You will begin to develop skills in writing, oral communication and team building which are important in business and industry today. You will learn how to set goals and make plans to insure that you attain those goals. You will learn research skills that will enable you to keep up with the informational demands of a technical career.

The specific goals of TEC 101 are:

- To provide students with an orientation to NEIT and the support services available to them.
- To provide students with an opportunity to evaluate their computer competencies and to learn how to use technology to access information.
- To encourage students to explore their career choice and the opportunities it provides.
- To encourage students to take responsibility for their own learning and develop personal management skills.

Your choice to attend New England Institute of Technology has proven that you have made a commitment to learn the theory and practical skills that you need to succeed in

TEC 101 has been designed to give you the tools that you need to succeed in your classes.

the high-tech workforce of the 21st century. The rapidly changing world of work requires that successful employees are highly skilled, able to work in teams, willing to make a commitment to lifelong learning and able to solve problems in practical and innovative ways. You'll learn all of these things during your time at New England Tech. TEC 101 lays the foundation for a successful and challenging technical career.

Reading: Rights, Responsibilities and Expectations of the College Experience

Introduction

The first quarter of college, although exciting, can be intimidating and overwhelming. There are so many choices and decisions to be made. Yet some people don't seem to have any problems. They get into the best classes with the best instructors, their schedule is the popular 9:00 a.m. to 1:00 p.m. on Mondays, Wednesdays, and Fridays, and they never have three hour breaks between classes, unless they work on campus. Oh yes, they always have the best jobs on campus, their financial aid papers come through in plenty of time, and they are never late to class because of child care problems. Upon graduation all of their credits are assured of transferring to the university of their choice, and their advisors are always available whenever they need an appointment! Perhaps I'm exaggerating a bit, but it does seem that one part of the student population has smooth sailing as they embark upon this voyage called the college experience, while others have choppy waters, typhoon winds, and shipwreck in store for them quarter after quarter. As counselors and educators who have navigated these waters ourselves and for thousands of other students in your situation, we would like to give you some maps to guide you around the rough spots and warn you about some potential ship sinkers.

We will explore some of your expectations about college, and the college's expectations of you. We will let you know your rights and responsibilities as students, as well as the rights and responsibilities of your instructors. We will discuss the variety of campus re-

From *The Community College: A New Beginning,* Second Edition by Aguilar et al. © 1998 by Kendall/Hunt Publishing Company.

sources available to you. I know that you might have thought this topic sounded like something to read when you can't fall asleep at night. Although the topic doesn't seem like it will be a Stephen King thriller, this is the stuff that those other students know and use to their advantage. You thought they were just lucky, but luck actually has nothing to do with being a successful student. We hope you begin to realize that more and more as you go through this orientation course.

Expectations

Why are you attending college? What do you expect to gain from your classes? A degree, you say. But why do you want a degree? Do you know what is involved in the process of acquiring that degree? These are some questions you should be able to answer as you begin your journey through college. If you don't have any expectations, does that mean anything that happens will please you? Somehow, I don't think so. You've probably heard the saying, "You usually get about what you expect from life." Apply that to your college experience. You will get out of college about as much as you expect and are willing to put forth effort to achieve.

What the college expects of you as a student is spelled out in your college catalog and in your student handbook. You need to become familiar with all of these. Most people don't even read them, and that is a mistake. When you drive a car, you are expected to know the rules of the road. If you don't, and you get ticketed for violating one of the laws, it usually costs you time and money to go to court and pay the fine. Ignorance of the law is no excuse. In the same manner you are expected to know the rules of the school. If you don't know what the school expects of you it could end up costing you time and tuition money to rectify your mistakes.

Make sure you keep a copy of the current college catalog from your first quarter. That is your contract with the school and is legally binding as long as you are continuously enrolled. (Check with your school for this policy. Institutions differ on the definition of "continuous.") If the college changes degree requirements while you are still a student, you are only obligated to fulfill the requirements that existed when you started. Use the catalog whenever you need to review your credits and classes, when you register, and each time you meet with your advisor. The catalog also contains the following:

- college policies and procedures
- academic programs
- requirements for graduation
- course descriptions
- college calendar (including holidays, starting and ending dates for each quarter, withdrawal dates, registration dates)
- tuition and fees
- GPA requirements for good academic standing
- faculty and administration
- college departments
- academic grading policies

The student handbook is another source of valuable information about the college. It contains more details about programs and services, student organizations, college activities, and may have a list of offices on campus with business hours, room numbers and telephone extensions. Any other information you need to know is usually provided in this publication.

Instructor Expectations

Your individual instructor's expectations are contained in his/her course syllabus. You should get one for every course. The syllabus is your contract with that instructor. It should tell you the course objectives, the name(s) of the textbook(s), grading policies, special requirements, and give you a schedule of assignments. Most instructors distribute the syllabus during the first class period. That's why it's so important to be there for the first class. Some of the information given at that time will not be repeated later, but you will be held accountable for knowing it. Instructors expect you to keep track of your syllabus and follow the schedule, even it they never mention it again. The minimum expectations of most instructors are that you attend class on a regular basis, participate in class discussions and activities, complete your assignments on time, and take tests and examinations when they are given.

In college classes you will be held to much higher standards than you were in high school. You will be expected to study more and devote more time to doing homework. The typical rule is that you should spend at least two hours studying outside of class for every hour you spend in class. Often you are required to do more extensive readings of textbooks and/or supplemental (also called collateral) readings. In most courses a portion of your grade is based on writing assignments. These can range from journals or short papers to longer essays or even extensive term papers involving research. Many instructors ask that your work be typewritten, and always expect that it will be clean, neat, and well organized. Non-compliance could lower your grade. Late work may not be accepted at all. In college you are responsible for your learning. No one will remind you to complete your assignments or do your homework.

Student Expectations

When you thought about what you expected college to be like, did you consider the ways in which it is different from high school? Depending on your high school experience, college may be similar or it may be very different. Take a moment and brainstorm (generate ideas) a list of all the ways college may be different for you. We started with some examples.

- Tuition is charged
- You buy your own books
- You choose your school
- Each program has its own requirements

_____

_____

_____

_____

Your instructor may ask you to discuss your list with the other students in your class or group.

Student Concerns about Starting College

Starting college can cause a certain amount of fear or apprehension. If you were not a strong student in high school or if you have been out of school for a number of years, you may be nervous about your study skills and your ability to do college level work. Other people worry about relationships and personal problems that will arise. Going to school requires a definite time commitment for attending classes and studying. Significant others may not understand that you are going to be busier than you were before. Child care arrangements and employment schedules may be more complicated than ever. There will be financial considerations, especially if you are not working or have changed from full time to part time employment while you are in college.

What are some of your fears or problems associated with you being in college?

Student Rights

As college students and adults you have certain rights that go beyond those of high school students. In high school many of the decisions were made for you. Sometimes you even felt like a second class citizen. Now that you are taking total responsibility for your education you are also entitled to know your rights.

A. You have the right to be treated with dignity and respect by your fellow students and all college employees.

That means everyone from the president of the college to the campus police; from your instructors to the bookstore clerks and cafeteria workers.

B. You have the right to receive a quality education.

Many colleges are even going so far as to issue educational guarantees. For example, if you get an academic degree (Associate of Arts or Associate of Science) from a community college, it will transfer to the public universities in your state. If you get a vocational degree (Associate in Applied Science) you should have the skills to get a job in your field. If your employer doesn't think you have the minimum skills necessary to do the job after you have completed a certain course of study, the college will pay the tuition for you to repeat the course(s).

C. You have the right to pursue your education in an environment that is safe and conducive to learning.

Usually the campus has a security or police department to insure that students, their cars, and their belongings are safe. While they cannot promise that nothing will ever get stolen from your car, or that your book bag will remain untouched if you leave it in the cafeteria for two hours, they are routinely patrolling the parking lots and buildings on campus. Many departments have security cameras that allow an officer to monitor all of the parking lots and building entrances at once. Other duties of the campus police include parking, traffic regulations, vehicle stickers, fire safety, escort services, as well as crime prevention. Many security offices also assist students by presenting crime awareness programs, and publishing the campus crime statistics. You have a right to know the amount and nature of crimes that are committed on campus.

An environment that is conducive to learning is one that is free of sexual harassment or any other behavior that is unwelcome, degrading, destructive and unnecessary. Most schools do have written policies regarding sexual harassment stating what is and is not acceptable behavior, and the disciplinary action for what is not acceptable. Everyone must be made aware of these policies, which are usually in the college catalog and student handbook. Be sure that your behavior is appropriate, and do not allow someone else to violate acceptable standards.

D. You have the right to your own opinion.

Although others in the class or on campus may not share your views, you have all of the constitutional rights to freedom of speech and expression. Remember, though, this does not give you the right to monopolize class time voicing your opinion.

E. You have the right to have your privacy respected.

The Family Educational Rights and Privacy Act (FERPA) is a federal law that gives you the right to know what is contained in your school records. It also protects the privacy of your records. Without your permission the college cannot give out information about your schedule, grades, academic standing, test scores, and such, even to your parents or spouse. That is the reason you must request in writing when you want your transcripts or placement test scores sent to another school. The college is allowed to issue directory information (name, address, etc.), but many schools today will not even release that information, especially over the phone. If you do not wish information about yourself given out, you can request that the college not provide this directory information to anyone.

F. You have the right to seek guidance.

The college offers academic advisors in every major to assist students with educational planning. Even if you are a part time student and were not assigned an advisor, you can request one. The counselors in the Office of Student Support Services are another source of advice on educational and career planning. They can also help with limited personal issues.

G. You have the right to express concern or dissatisfaction with any situation that impedes your pursuit of education.

Find out what the grievance procedures are on your campus. Follow through until your problem is resolved. Remember, there are levels of authority in any institution. Usually the best results are obtained when you follow the chain of command.

H. You have the right to withdraw from any course until the withdrawal deadline date.

I. You have the right to a final course review if you feel the instructor's final grade for the course has not been fair.

Contact the instructor first to see if you can solve the problem at that level. If not, go to the department chairperson. Follow the procedure outlined in your catalog or handbook.

Student Responsibilities

One reason some students do not do well in college is they do not fully understand their responsibilities. Although many of my students enjoy the increased freedoms of being in college, they seem to forget that increased responsibilities come with the package deal. They still have that high school mind set that the school is responsible for everything from student behavior to how much one learns. I can't tell you how many times I've heard the complaint, "**They** didn't teach me anything at that school."

In college there is definitely a shift, or transferring of responsibility to the student as an adult in charge of his/her own life. Consider yourself a consumer (paying customer) of your education. You have paid for these classes; it is up to you to see that you get your money's worth. What are some of the major responsibilities college students need to assume?

A. It is your responsibility to recognize and respect the rights of other students.

Talk softly in study areas or near classes that are in session. Be quiet in the library, and return your books when they are due. Don't damage magazines that others will need to use. If you are able bodied be sure to give priority use of the designated elevators and rest rooms to persons with disabilities. They don't have the option of using the stairs or other facilities.

B. It is your responsibility to treat others with dignity and respect.

In class discussions listen to what others have to say and don't make fun of someone else's remarks. Respect your instructors and fellow students. Don't disrupt the class by chatting with the person next to you during the lecture. It is also disruptive to the instructor and the rest of the class when students "pack-up" 10 to 15 minutes before the end of the period. It is obvious they think there won't be anything of importance said. Some even put their coats on and sit on the edge of their chairs, ready to bolt out of the room the second class is dismissed. This behavior is rude, but it is also self-defeating because the end of the period is when the instructor gives instructions for an assignment, reviews hints for the test, or provides other helpful information.

C. You are responsible for your behavior on campus.

Be responsible to clean up your own mess, don't litter, smoke only in the designated areas, don't steal from others, obey the laws for driving and parking, act in a mature, adult manner in classrooms, student lounge areas, and hallways.

D. It is your responsibility to ask when you do not understand something or when you need help.

For example, if you need special services or tutoring, it is up to you to contact the appropriate department or program. You should make appointments to see your advisor for registration or academic planning. Don't wait for someone else to call you first. You may never get what you need.

E. It is your responsibility to attend and participate in class.

The attendance policy will vary with each course and each instructor. Many college students believe they can make their own decisions about whether or not to attend class. This is always a bad idea. Some instructors may allow you to miss class occasionally for good reason, but think about all that you are going to miss by not being there. A large percentage of the material you will be required to know from the class comes from the lecture. If you know in advance that you cannot attend or if you are ill and must miss a class, notify the instructor. Do whatever you can to make up the work. Submit any assignments due that day. Remember, too, that you paid to take this class. You are throwing away your money when you are not attending.

F. If the instructor is late for class it is your responsibility to wait at least 10 to 15 minutes before you leave.

Everyone has emergencies and anyone can be tied up in traffic, so it is only common courtesy to wait. Should the instructor come after you have left, you will be responsible for the missed material.

G. It is your responsibility to do your homework assignments and turn them in on time.

You are also responsible to be aware of what the assignments are, in other words, to read the syllabus.

H. It is your responsibility to read class materials.

Students must read materials in order to be prepared to ask and answer questions, participate in discussions, and to offer comments in class.

I. It is your responsibility to be an active learner.

This is your education. You have to take the initiative to learn, even if the instructor is boring, unfair, not cool, doesn't like you, etc. Failing a course because you don't like the instructor hurts only yourself. Regardless of who the teacher is, it is your responsibility to do the assignments and go to class prepared to learn.

J. It is your responsibility to be aware of college policies and procedures and the chain of command.

When you have a problem to resolve, it is most effective to follow through with the person who has the authority to implement the solution.

K. Some policies that are a must to know:

1. Course prerequisites. These are found in the catalog.

2. Payment policies and deadline dates.

3. Course withdrawal procedures and deadline dates. These are described in the catalog and handbook.

4. Instructor requirements, including attendance policies. You will find this in the course syllabus.

5. Academic, Financial, and Veterans' Standards of Progress. See the college catalog and/or get this information from the financial aid and veterans offices.

6. Major/graduation requirements. These are in the college catalog.

7. Appeals processes. Once again, the catalog is the place to look for this.

L. You are responsible for knowing the information in the Student Handbook and for managing your behavior accordingly.

M. It is your responsibility as a student to try to understand another person's perspectives.

Just as you have the right to speak your mind, you have the responsibility to allow others to do the same. Everyone will not think the same way on any given issue. One of the purposes of education is to get you to think with an open mind, to evaluate what you see and hear, and to develop and use logic and reasoning skills.

N. It is your responsibility to provide thoughtful feedback to instructors on evaluations.

Fill out the course evaluation as honestly and thoroughly as you can whenever you are asked to do so. Add written comments. Your instructors will value your opinion if you are constructive in your critique. They may improve their teaching techniques to benefit future students.

O. It is your responsibility NOT to develop bad habits.

Students should not talk during class, chew gum, eat, or drink noisily, be late for class, create a disturbance, sleep during class, cut classes, be unprepared, not pay attention, or be apathetic.

P. You are responsible for checking your progress with your instructors.

You may be given a midterm report, but it is usually not required by the college. It is up to the students to keep track of grades received on assignments, tests, and quizzes. For an accurate report, make an appointment to meet with the teacher in his/her office to see how you are doing.

Q. It is your responsibility to evaluate your time commitments and manage your schedule accordingly.

Everyone has things they must do. It is up to you, however, not to schedule doctor, dentist, haircut or other appointments that will conflict with your class time. You will also need to plan for homework and study time in addition to the hours you spend in class. The more roles you have, the more difficult this will be. But, it is not the instructor's fault if you wait to do an assignment until the night before it is due, then get called in unexpectedly to work overtime and can't get the assignment done on time.

R. It is your responsibility to accept the consequences if you do not do what you should.

The buck stops with you.

Instructor Rights

Since there are two parties in the teacher/learner relationship, we thought it would be appropriate to acquaint you with the rights and responsibilities of your instructors. The status given to faculty may vary from campus to campus, and full time teachers may have more influence than part timers, but overall they have some basic assumptions about what should happen. These are things that you should understand as well.

A. Instructors have the right to expect students to arrive on time.

It is distracting and annoying to have your train of thought interrupted every time someone else enters the room. Some teachers will close and lock the door to prevent people from entering late. Others may not be quite that strict, but will appreciate a latecomer slipping in as quietly as possible.

B. Instructors have the right to expect students to behave as adults.

Students should pay attention in class, listen and take notes, not disturb the class by talking with friends, getting up, walking around, or leaving early. If you must leave early it is best to mention this to the instructor before class. If you have a disability that necessitates you moving around, let your instructor know in advance. It is perfectly acceptable for you to accommodate your needs, but this should not come as a total surprise to the instructor.

C. Instructors have the right to expect respect from students.

It should never be necessary to shout, use obscenities, or in any other way show disrespect to a teacher. If there is a severe problem that cannot be resolved with the instructor, talk to the department chairperson or the provost.

D. Instructors have the right to be notified if students have a problem or concern about their courses.

They should not have to hear about it first from the president of the college or their department chairperson. Always use your instructor as the first resort to seek a solution for any class problem.

E. Instructors have the right to expect students to read the syllabus, to be prepared for class, and to be prepared for tests.

(Bring your own pencils, etc.)

F. Instructors have the right to expect students to seek help during posted office hours, to request make-up materials, or to check on work missed during an absence.

It is really unfair of students to expect the teacher to be a walking file cabinet, carrying all of the handouts from the last three sessions, just in case someone didn't get them or lost their copies. Many teachers have their classes scheduled back to back and in different rooms, which really makes it inconvenient to stay after class to talk to a student who missed a previous session.

G. Instructors have the right not to be expected to calculate grades in their heads or on the spot just because the student caught them in the cafeteria or parking lot.

Even if the teacher has his/her grade book at hand, don't expect to look over his/her shoulder at your grades; that's a breech of confidentiality if other students' grades are on the same page.

H. Instructors have the right of academic freedom.

As degreed professionals they are granted the right to express themselves freely (within the college's code of conduct), to conduct their classes as they see fit, to assign homework, to use outside sources of information as provided by the copyright laws, and determine their own system for grading.

Instructor Responsibilities

Your instructors have certain responsibilities to you as students and to the college. Because they seem somewhat self explanatory, we will not go into great detail about each. Here is a list of several that we thought were important.

It is your instructor's responsibility:

A. To arrive and start class on time.

B. To inform the students in advance if he/she knows class will be cancelled.

C. To cover the material in the syllabus.

D. To treat students and their opinions with respect.

E. To inform students of their progress without violating confidentiality.

F. To provide a learning environment.

G. To present effective lectures that stick to the subject without rambling.

H. To be prepared and organized.

I. To be considerate of the able bodied and the disabled student, i.e., not speaking too fast or in a monotone, leaving transparencies or visual aids on the screen long enough to take notes, and willingly providing reasonable accommodations for students with disabilities.

J. To explain concepts, and to repeat or reteach if necessary.

K. To be in their office during posted office hours and to keep scheduled appointments.

L. Not to:

1. keep class beyond the end of the period

2. show partiality or favoritism

3. embarrass students

4. behave as if their class is the only class the student is taking

5. behave as if their opinion is the only opinion

■ Summary

- New England Institute of Technology has a long history of educating individuals so that they can become productive members of the workforce.
- The New England Institute of Technology's mission and educational philosophy illustrates its commitment to providing an education to students of differing abilities.
- TEC 101 was designed to prepare students to succeed in college so that they can succeed in their careers.
- As a college student, you must take responsibility for your own education.

Additional Resources

Resources in the Learning Resources Center (call numbers are shown in parentheses after the citation):

Ludden, L. L. (1996). *Back to school: a college guide for adults*. Indianapolis, IN: Park Avenue. (LC5251 .L84 1996)

Saunders, D. (Ed.). (1994). *The complete student handbook*. Cambridge, MA: Blackwell. (LB2343.3 .C655 1994)

Web Site:

New England Institute of Technology: http://mypipeline.neit.edu

Activities

1-1 Use the Class List to record the telephone numbers, addresses and E-mail addresses of each member of the class.

1-2 Read the TEC 101 syllabus.

1-3 Write three questions that you have about the syllabus.

1-4 Be prepared to discuss these questions at the next class meeting.

Activity 1-1.

		Class List		
Name	Tech	Address	Telephone Number	E-Mail Address

■ Activity 1-3.

Questions About the TEC 101 Syllabus

Write three questions that you have about the TEC 101 syllabus.

1.

2.

3.

CHAPTER 2
Setting Goals

"New England Tech has given me the chance to advance into areas of business that were not possible before. I am employed as a sales consultant and really enjoy my work. The lessons I learned at NEIT go beyond the classroom; I have learned that hard work pays off. You get back what you invest . . . invest well and receive success. One has to be self-disciplined to succeed."

Lynne DeBoer
Business Management Technology

Chapter Designers:

Mary Jean Clapp, Associate Professor of Computer and Network Servicing
    Technology
Catherine Kennedy, Vice President for Career Development
Margaret McKenna, Assistant Professor, Chair of Electrical Technology
Ann M. Ricci, Assistant Professor of Administrative Medical Assistant Technology
Peter R. Schuyler, Associate Professor of Electronics Engineering Technology
Thomas P. Strolla, Assistant Professor of Video & Radio Production Technology

What Students Are Saying . . .

"I learned a lot in my TEC 101 class and I liked it. I learned how to organize my time better. Even though I am attending school and working full-time, I still managed to get my work done in all of my classes and this class helped me to stay motivated and to keep me going when I felt tired and felt like I couldn't go anymore."

Victor Lopes
Computer and Network Servicing Technology

In This Chapter

You will

- Learn how to set personal, educational and career goals.
- Develop an action plan and time line to meet these goals.

■ Introduction

One of the keys to managing a busy life filled with multiple priorities is to set goals and plan your time. Why should you establish goals? When you get into your car to drive somewhere it makes no sense to leave without knowing your final destination. So why would you want to embark on a career and a life without having a destination? Goals are life "destinations," so it makes a lot of sense to start on your life's journey with a destination and a map. Setting goals helps you to determine where you want to go in life. Developing action plans and time lines provides the map to get there.

This chapter will help you to understand the importance of identifying career and educational goals and creating an action plan and time line to help you to achieve those goals. Goals allow you to measure your success and evaluate your strategies for getting there. Action plans and time lines help you to establish how and when you will achieve your goals. Time management tools and techniques presented in this chapter will help you to maintain the proper balance of professional, educational and personal goals so that you can achieve success.

■ Setting Career, Educational and Personal Goals

First, let's look at how to establish goals. Where do you want to be in five years? In ten years? By seriously thinking about this now, you can start formulating a plan to make sure that you do what is necessary to reach your ultimate goals. Think about what matters to *you* because these are *your* goals. Discard what your family or friends or people on the street may want you to become and focus on what you want out of life. Start imagining what your life will be in the future and work toward planning the steps involved to get there.

Once you have determined your ultimate goal, you can begin planning long- and short-term goals to help you get where you need to be. Long-term goals take several years to a lifetime to accomplish. Short-term goals make up all of the steps in between. Goals help you to assess your progress, keep you on track and remind you of what is important.

GOALS

Provide you with specific direction and a means to measure your success.

Let you visualize your success and give you a sense of accomplishment.

Are composed of structured, action-oriented strategies on a time line.

Nurture self-motivation and self-assessment.

There are three types of goals:

- Career—attainment of a position that interests and challenges you and provides adequate compensation to maintain your lifestyle
- Educational—achievement in college, attainment of degrees or intellectual pursuits
- Personal—life achievement, family, artistic pursuits, hobbies or avocations

For the purpose of the activities in this chapter, we will focus on career and educational goals since they apply more specifically to the material presented in this course. There are three parts to a sensible, well-stated goal:

- *What*—is your goal?
- *When*—(by what date) do you want to accomplish that goal?
- *How*—are you going to do it?

By answering these questions, you are starting to form a plan to accomplish your goals. As an example, your long-term educational and career goals may be to graduate from college and get a good position in the field that you studied. That combined goal can be broken down into a number of intermediate educational and career goals. These intermediate goals may include succeeding in specific courses, securing an internship in the field that you have chosen, putting together a quality resume and portfolio and obtaining a good job after a successful interview. Each of these pieces helps make up the *what* of your goals. Then, those goals can be divided into very specific tasks that make up the *when* and *how* of goal-setting.

It is helpful to see goals as a series of specific tasks. By breaking goals down into smaller tasks, it is easier to keep track of your progress and stay motivated by being able to accomplish portions of your larger goal on a regular basis. Goals should be reasonable, realistic and planned within a time period that allows you to achieve some balance in your life. Once you have decided on some basic goals, assign priorities to them depending on which are the most important to accomplish now.

There are just a few more things to think about before you start formulating an action plan to achieve your goals. When you first begin to set goals, you may very likely set them too high or too low. Goals are tools that will help you to achieve all that you want to achieve. They should be adjusted and updated as you become more keenly aware of your abilities and your capacity to carry out a plan. As you get more practice setting goals, it will be easier for you to set goals that are both challenging and realistically attainable.

If you set your goals unrealistically high, you will become frustrated if you are unable to achieve them. Remember that you are human and give yourself the opportunity to make mistakes and learn from them. You will not always be at your best and conditions

Use your successes and failures as a learning experience.

may not always be right for you to achieve your optimum performance. On the other hand, don't set your goals too low either. There is little satisfaction in accomplishing something that was very easy to do or did not challenge your abilities.

So, what *should* you do if you fail? Take this as an opportunity to assess your failure and determine the cause. It may be that your goal was unrealistic. It could also be that you did not allow adequate time to complete the tasks. The failure could also mean that you did not put enough effort into attaining that goal. On the positive side, what should you do if you succeed? If your success required very little effort, your goal may not have been high enough. If your success was achieved through concentration and hard work, then reward yourself for a job well done. In either case, use your successes and failures as a learning experience and as a means to better define your goals in the future.

■ Developing an Action Plan and Time Line

Once you have determined what your goals are, you can begin creating an action plan made up of the steps needed to accomplish those goals. An action plan should be very specific. It should include an action or strategy to achieve the goal, a statement of how that action can be carried out, the time it will take to complete each action and a projected date or time when an action should be completed.

The sample action plan on the next page outlines some of the steps necessary to achieve the short-term educational goal of completing the quarter with a grade point average (GPA) of 3.5. The first column lists specific actions or strategies that will help to accomplish the goal of getting a good GPA. In this case, the plan includes rearranging a work schedule, creating a time line for completing assignments, organizing a study group, improving reading skills and preparing well for class.

Do you have time to waste?

Having an Action Plan helps keep you on track when there are things around to distract you.

In the second column, there are specific notes about how to complete each strategy. This column should identify the skills, materials, information or help that might be needed to carry out this portion of the plan. The third column includes the estimated time it will take to accomplish each part of the plan. The final column gives a projected day or time when each part of the plan should be complete. As you can see, this sample action plan includes a number of clearly-defined tasks which can be accomplished within a reasonable time frame.

The sample action plan for a long-term career goal is quite similar. Since this is a long-term goal, many of the actions require a number of separate steps (listed in the How column). It may also take more time to carry out each of the items in the How column. Copies of a blank Action Plan and Time Line Toward Graduation are in the Appendix.

Sample Short-Term Goal—Educational Type

Action Plan

Short-Term Goal: I will complete this quarter with a GPA of 3.5.

Action/Strategy (Be Specific)	How	Time Invested	When Completed
Reorganize my work schedule to move five of my weekday hours to the weekend.	Speak with my supervisor.	30 minutes	Monday prior to the start of the quarter
Create a Time Line for the completion of my assignments.	Review the due dates for my assignments on my class syllabus. Create a schedule for my school assignments as well as my personal and work commitments.	1 to 1½ hours	Friday of week one
Identify three other students in my class with similar schedules and form a study group.	Ask my instructor to give the class 15 minutes to form study groups.	15 minutes	Second class meeting
Improve my reading skills.	Attend two workshops in the Academic Skills Center to improve my reading skills.	2 hours	By Friday of week one and two
Prepare for my weekly lecture class.	Read assignment prior to the class meeting. Discuss information in reading assignment with study group prior to and following class.	1 hour per day	By Monday evening of each week

Sample Long-Term Goal—Career Type

Action Plan

Long-Term Goal: I will be gainfully employed in my profession following my graduation from NEIT.

Action/Strategy (Be Specific)	How	Time Invested	When Completed
I will identify career opportunities that I will pursue upon graduation.	I will search the web for, and communicate with, two professional organizations related to the _____ technology.	6–8 hours	
	I will search the web and the LRC for professional publications related to the _____ technology.	2 hours	
	I will meet with Career Services for an initial interview and two follow-up visits to get the assistance I will need to plan my career search.	2–3 hours	
	I will search the telephone book (hard copy or web) for local organizations affiliated with the _____ technology.	30 minutes	

Reading: Time Management

Introduction

"Time is the one thing they're not making any more of . . ."

Radio commercial for LaSalle Bank

When you hear the phrase "time management," do you envision yourself enslaved to a desk calendar, wall calendar, pocket calendar, computer scheduler, pocket watch? Do you see yourself hurrying to finish one task so you can start the next one "on schedule?" Do you daydream about mountains of "to-do" lists piled high on your desk; or are you, in your mind's eye, rushing to catch a train, briefcase in hand?

Effective time management does involve some physical scheduling tools, simply because most of us find it easier to retrieve information from a piece of paper (or software) than from the filing system in our minds. However, arbitrary schedules and lists won't do a thing for you until you've come to grips with the two factors that keep time under control: **Priorities** and **Commitment**.

In this chapter we'll look at strategies for turning your long- and short-term goals into priority statements. A question that will weave through our discussion is "What's the best possible use of my time RIGHT NOW?" We'll introduce you to some scheduling tools that will turn the abstract "goal" into simple steps toward "action." Contrary to those mental pictures of lists and clocks, you'll learn how scheduling can actually bring you more free time and less guilt!

We'll also talk about the concept of commitment: ways to motivate yourself to stay with your scheduling plan, and hints for conquering disorganization, procrastination and distractions. We'll also offer some hints from time management "experts"—useful ways to get control of your most difficult time-related challenges.

From *The Community College: A New Beginning*. Second Edition by Aguilar et al. © 1998 by Kendall/Hunt Publishing Company.

Pretest

Purpose: To help you find areas to improve as you handle the responsibility of scheduling your own time as a college student.

A. How much time per week do you believe you devote to the following activities?

Activity	# Hours Per Week
1. Attending class	_____
2. Studying/reading/doing homework	_____
3. Working at a job	_____
4. Watching TV	_____
5. Sleeping	_____
6. Personal care (bathing, hair, etc.)	_____
7. Hobbies	_____
8. Shopping	_____
9. Eating	_____
10. Being with friends	_____
11. On the phone	_____
12. Other _____	_____

TOTAL HRS. = _____

B. Have any of the following happened to you since you started college?

	Yes	No
1. Overslept and missed/late to class	_____	_____
2. Forgot to do an assignment	_____	_____
3. Chose to go out with friends and didn't complete an assignment	_____	_____
4. Asked an instructor for a deadline extension	_____	_____
5. Got your work schedule mixed up	_____	_____
6. Missed or was late to class due to transportation problem	_____	_____
7. Skipped class for no particular reason	_____	_____

New Outlook on Time

You have probably already noticed that the way you use your time in college is much different from the way you used it in high school. In college, you are expected to be much more responsible for your own time scheduling. For example:

1. In college, many courses do not meet every day. You must keep track of class meeting times yourself.

2. Many college instructors do not take attendance. If you miss class, you will have a vague awareness that your grades will suffer, but attendance is up to you.

3. Usually "homework" is not turned in on a class-by-class basis, but assignments are more long-term. They require more sophisticated scheduling to be completed on time. The same is true for studying for tests—preparation is a more long-term project.

4. College work is demanding. You need to plan to study two hours outside of class for every hour in class. So if you're carrying 15 credit hours, your total time commitment is 45 hours—the equivalent of a full time job.

5. Your parents are less likely to keep tabs on your assignments; and your friends are more likely to come up with tempting activities to distract you from your studies.

So, as you can see, going to college is very much about committing large blocks of time to this endeavor. Those whose lives include multiple commitments (job, children, athletics) find the time pressure even more intense. You need to have a clear picture of why you're devoting so much time to this college thing—what is it exactly you're hoping to accomplish?

Setting Your Goals

Goals come in two main types: long-term and short-term. For the purpose of this example, we're going to state a long-term goal for everybody as follows:

"To obtain my associate's degree within 6 quarters, spending only the funds from my part-time and summer jobs."

A goal statement must define a realistic, measurable goal in words: "obtain my associate's degree;" be clearly attached to a time frame: "within 6 quarters;" and identify the costs involved: "spending only the funds from my part-time and summer jobs." Complete Activity 2-1 to become more efficient at setting goals.

After you've taken a look at some of your goals and their relationship to your college education, you will see that time management is directly related to your goals. Now, examine the obvious priorities that are suggested by the goals that are part of your life. When you break down your goals, long-term to short-term, step by step, you become aware of activities that fall into the following three categories:

1. **Urgent**—Things that have forced themselves to the top of your pile by virtue of an impending deadline. Examples: finish an assignment due tomorrow, take out the garbage if tomorrow is collection day, go to work, attend class.

2. **Responsibilities**—Things that lead up to the completion of tasks which may or may not have a deadline; hopefully before they reach the level of "Urgent." Examples: prepare meals, call Mom, take the car in for service, make an appointment for advising, go to the library to research a paper.

3. **Relaxation**—Recreational activities which require "free time," that is, free of the pressure of being either a "Responsibility" or an "Urgency." Examples: clean your room, watch TV, read a book. You will notice that even some of these can become "Urgent" in your life if they are attached to a time-frame event.

An awareness of these categories can help you answer the very important question, "What is the best possible use of my time RIGHT NOW?" You need to know how many "urgent" tasks you have in front of you, and how much time you must devote to "responsibilities" to keep them under control. You also begin to learn that you can't enjoy "relaxation" activities when deadlines are looming in the other areas. For instance, have you ever given in to the temptation to go to the movies with a friend, only to "remember" when you got home that you had a math test the next morning? To make matters worse, you'd missed two classes when you took off on that impromptu ski trip three weeks ago, and you never got around to asking anyone for the notes. Now it's midnight—no, 1:00 a.m.—and calling someone in your class for math notes feels a bit risky.

This scenario is the result of several factors: trusting your memory to keep track of "responsibilities" and "urgent" deadlines, not having a focus on your goals so you don't know what the priorities are, and making a decision on the spur of the moment to let "recreational" desires come before your goals. Hey . . . don't beat yourself up about it; it's human nature! But let's get it under control.

Reasons to Get a College Education

1. Statistics show the salary of the average college graduate is 33–50% higher than that of the average high school grad. This is true for both men and women.

2. Women college graduates are better able to support themselves, if need be, and have more opportunity to choose their own hours during the child-raising years.

3. Studies consistently show that each decade there has been an increase in the percentage of jobs that require some training beyond high school. This trend is expected to continue.

4. In recent years, America has seen a layoff crisis (downsizing, early retirement). It is easier to be flexible, mobile, and re-train for other occupations if you have a college education behind you. If you are trained to do just one job, as in the case of many high school grads, you'll find it tougher to be re-employed.

5. College graduates enjoy more prestige and respect in the community.

6. There are many other personal reasons: personal dreams, desire for a higher caliber of friends, desire to attend those cool homecoming games as a "real" alum . . .

Where do you see yourself in 10 years?

Hold in your mind a picture of yourself: (your job, your lifestyle, the house you live in, the clothes you wear) in ten years if you continue your education and finish your degree. Now, get a mental picture of yourself having dropped out and having no degree. Which picture is prettier?

Advice from the Experts

Here are some helpful tips from a few of the thousands of books that have been written about Time Management:

1. **Pam Young & Peggy Jones,** The Side-tracked Home Executive: *Break down big tasks into small ones (things that take less than ten minutes). Use small blocks of time to do these tasks. Write the tasks on index cards, and when you accomplish one, move its card to the back of the box to get a feeling of accomplishment.*

2. **Alan Lakein,** How to Get Control of Your Time and Your Life: *Start with your major goal in life, the one you think of as your "MISSION IN LIFE." We all have one, even if we haven't defined it in words. Make lists of tasks to be done, then prioritize each task A, B, or C. Do the A's first, the B's as you can, and forget about the C's.*

3. **Stephanie Culp,** How to Get Organized When You Don't Have the Time: *Have a designated place for every item you own. Get control of paper by handling every paper that comes to you only once—decide then and there what to do with it, and do it.*

4. **James T. McCoy,** The Management of Time: *Divide all the tasks on your "to-do" list into "Have to" and "Should do." The dividing line is the following question: "Will my work, co-workers, or my family suffer in any significant way if I fail to do this today?" If the answer is "No," it's a "Should do," and can safely be left until tomorrow—or next week.*

5. **William Oncken, Jr.,** Managing Management Time: *The best part of this book is the appendix called "Collected Sayings of Ben Franklin's Grandfather." One example: "Our Maker gave us TIME to keep everything from happening at once."*

6. **Dave Ellis,** Becoming a Master Student:
   1. *Be aware of your best, most productive time of day.*
   2. *Avoid marathon study sessions.*
   3. *Learn to say NO.*
   4. *Accept less than perfection when perfection is not required.*
   5. *Try, when you are getting ready to quit for the day, to do "just one more thing."*

7. **Tim Walter and Al Siebert,** Student Success: How to Succeed in College and Still Have Time for Your Friends: *You may have heard it said, "If you want something done, ask a busy person." It does seem that the busiest, most involved students accomplish the most and get the best grades. That's because the busier you are, the more you MUST rely on scheduling tools, and those tools really do work.*

8. **Benjamin Franklin:** *"Dost thou love life, then do not squander time, for that's the stuff life is made of."*

The Spoilers: Procrastination and Distraction

Dealing with Procrastination

Everybody procrastinates at one time or another. Why? Two reasons: *inertia* and *avoidance.*

Inertia is probably the easiest type of procrastination to overcome. You remember from science class that inertia simply means "a body once in motion tends to remain in motion, and a body stationary tends to remain stationary." So, if *your* body is tending to remain stationary (for instance, in front of the TV or under the covers), you can use a few simple tricks to get your body into the "in motion" category. Once again, begin by asking yourself the age-old question, "What is the best possible use of my time RIGHT NOW?"

Before your brain has a chance to tell you, "Sleeping is good," get a grip on your priorities. What's urgent? NAME IT! Look at your Action Plan, if it applies, or ask yourself what the very first step is in the direction of that goal or "urgency."

Special Time Management Situations

Some students have more challenges than average, because of their lifestyles or circumstances. Here are some brief tips to help meet those extra time-management challenges:

1. Part-time students with full-time jobs:

You need to pay particular attention to the concept of dividing your time into blocks or chunks, and be certain to schedule in time for unexpected emergencies at work or at home. Your health and rest are of utmost importance; be especially careful of overextending yourself so that you are unable to get enough sleep. You probably need to decide which is your top priority—school or work—and if necessary, adjust the time frame of your goal to take fewer classes at a time. If you take more than one class at a time, ask your advisor to help you choose classes that are "balanced," for example don't take Chemistry and Calculus in the same semester.

2. Moms (or Dads) going to school and raising kids and running a home:

There's probably no one else in the world who needs time management skills more than you do. You need time for household chores, shopping, cooking, getting the kids to school and activities on time, helping with kids' homework, listening to problems and drying tears, doing your own studying, getting to class . . . the list goes on and on. Say, do you get to have a life, too? There is so much stress in this situation, sometimes you will be tempted to think it isn't worth it. Two hints for you: First, get a very firm grip on your goals. Why are you seeking that degree? What improvements will it make in your life and the lives of your loved ones? If you can see this clearly, it will make all the difference when things look bleakest. Second, everybody has to have a schedule, not just you. The scheduling tools include activities of each family member, and you can then remind and encourage each other. Also, try to find a friend at school who is in the same situation. That support can be crucial for both of you.

3. Students with health problems:

Once again, your health must be your top priority, even if it means slowing down the achievement of your goals by taking fewer classes at once. Whether you have a chronic illness or a disability, you need to schedule in time for rest, physical therapy, proper nutrition, visits to the doctor, etc. before you schedule your class and study time. Be realistic about what you can handle. If you become ill during

the semester, don't just stop going to class. See your instructor and try to work out time to catch up, or ask for an Incomplete grade which you can finish the following semester.

4. Multiple commitments:

Athletes, musicians, etc. If part of your reason for attending college is the opportunity it affords you to play your sport or perform using your talents, you need to consider your activity and your education as equally important. If eligibility is an issue, naturally you are going to want to keep your grades up. Your best bet is to rely on the "buddy system" with a teammate or friend who is in the same situation. Hold each other accountable for maintaining a wise study and practice schedule. Obviously, not enough can be said about picking out the right person for your "buddy." The guy who thinks it won't hurt to party on school nights is probably not the "buddy" to choose.

5. Overcommitment:

Full time school and work, too many activities, etc. What's your priority? We repeat, what's your priority? Get a firm vision of where you want to be in, say, five years. If you are working full time and going to school full time, your grades are going to suffer. You are going to be tired. You are not going to have time for relaxation or social activities. The same is true if you have committed yourself to too many activities. It's great to take advantage of the opportunities college has to offer for sports, music, theater, clubs, and new friends. But to handle your goal-related responsibilities, you just have to decide which of these activities you can't live without, and pass on the rest.

6. Personal problems:

When you are in college, the rest of your life doesn't just stop. You will fall prey to personal pitfalls of all kinds: emotional, relationship-related, or financial to name a few. If you find yourself overwhelmed by a personal problem while the semester is in progress, take advantage of your school's counselors. They are there to help, they've seen it all before, and most of them are easy to talk to and have lots of ideas to help you through. There is no better wisdom than knowing when you need help and asking for it. Don't even wait until it gets out of hand—go today!

Eight Easy Time Management Tips

1. Ask yourself: "What's the best possible use of my time RIGHT NOW?"

2. Schedule time for relaxation and enjoyable activities.

3. Don't be afraid to ask for help if things get stressful (delegate tasks, reduce work load, ask for extended deadlines, talk to a counselor).

4. Take advantage of "waiting time" (carry a book, your calendar, note paper, balance your checkbook, plan your weekly meals).

5. Try getting up a half hour earlier. Commit to using that time productively (exercise, cook & freeze a meal, wash a load of clothes, re-read today's assignment).

6. Find a way to get a feeling of accomplishment when you finish a task (cross it off, move the card, reward yourself).

7. Identify the "very first step." Often all it takes to get us motivated and rolling on a plan is to define the very first action one has to take to put the plan in motion. Take the "very first step" and the others will follow more easily.

8. Keep a clear vision of your most important goal. Learn to daydream, seeing yourself and your life as it will be when that goal is attained.

What does your scheduling tool tell you you're supposed to be doing right now? For example, you have a term paper in the works. You have to finish the research today if you're going to meet the deadline. But you stayed up late last night and at 9:00 a.m., your stationary body wants to stay that way. What's the first step? If you can tell yourself, "If I get up and get in the shower," you will usually find that's enough to get you "in motion."

But suppose the problem is really *avoidance*? What if that reluctance to get going on the research paper stems from the notion that a) you chose the wrong topic and there's not enough research to support it, or b) the subject is too difficult and you feel you may not be able to tackle the paper successfully, or c) . . . a myriad of other self-defeating thoughts. There are many reasons why we procrastinate based on the desire to avoid something unpleasant. For instance:

1. Fear of failure, or not doing as well as we'd like

2. Fear of not being able to handle success

3. Desire to avoid particular people, relationships or situations

4. Desire to avoid an unpleasant task, like doing dishes or figuring taxes

5. Feeling overwhelmed by the size or scope of a task

6. Perfectionism—"If I can't make it perfect, why even start?"

7. Fear of someone else's judgement of your work

Handling *avoidance* type procrastination is pretty much similar to your approach to the inertia type. You still want to break down your dreaded task into its parts or steps, then tackle the very first step without worrying about the others. But to really overcome avoidance you have to deal with the emotional issues and mental attitudes that are getting in your way. It's easy for someone else to tell you to "feel confident"; but only you can get to the bottom of this! In the chart on the next page are some suggestions to help you.

Overcoming Distractions: Sara's Demolished Study Plan

Sara had planned to study Saturday afternoon, and had made detailed plans for how she would use her time to finish assignments for math, physics, literature, and music history. She needed to be finished studying by 5:00 p.m. since she had a date Saturday evening and she wanted enough time to look really hot. She planned to begin studying at 1:00, right after lunch.

Sara jumped into the car and ran down to Wendy's to get some chili for lunch. While there, she ran into her high school friend, Laura, whom she hadn't seen in a couple of months. They spent some time catching up—a lot of time, actually—and Sara didn't leave the restaurant until 1:30. On the way home she noticed she was nearly out of gas. She stopped at the gas station, and also checked out the mini-mart for some study-break snacks.

By the time Sara got home it was nearly 2:00. Sara had wanted to save some bucks while at community college, so she was still living at home. Sometimes her parents didn't realize that college studying was more time consuming than high school had been, and asked her to help out at home more often than Sara would like. Today, for instance, she arrived home and her mom asked her to please "keep an eye" on her little brother, age 10, so Mom could go shopping. Sara shoved a video into the VCR and told her brother to stay out of trouble while she studied.

Fifteen minutes into the literature reading assignment, the phone rang. It was the guy Sara was going out with that night, calling to ask if she'd rather see a movie or go to a dance club. They talked for a while, maybe twenty minutes, but after they hung up, Sara found it difficult to concentrate. She was really looking forward to the date.

After trying for a while to keep reading, Sara finally got up and went down to the kitchen for a soft drink. There she found the mess left after her brother had fixed himself a snack.

Procrastination Hints

1. Break the big tasks down into small steps. Schedule them, using your scheduling tools. Especially use your to-do list; it's motivating to see tasks checked off.

2. Find "step one" and start there without contemplating the rest of the project yet.

3. Set a time limit: "I'll work on step one (or two or ten) for 15 minutes." Sometimes you'll get involved and keep going.

4. Find a buddy to whom you'll agree to be accountable. Share your plan for tackling the project, and ask him to check up on you.

5. Suppose you missed something in class and the assignment doesn't make sense. You'll need to find a fellow student or ask the instructor for clarification. That, of course, would be your step one.

6. The trick is to train your mind that "When we sit here, it's time to study." Have all your materials ready, too, so you don't waste time looking for them.

7. Use positive self-talk. Remember Stuart Smalley on "Saturday Night Live"? "I'm good enough, I'm smart enough, and gosh darn it, people like me!" It was silly when "Stuart" did it, but actually the concept does work. Try to replace a negative thought with a positive one. Instead of, "I'll never get all this work done!", think, "I know I can at least read the chapter; I'll do that first."

8. It helps to hold out a carrot for yourself—something you will find really rewarding that you'll do for yourself after, say, reading three chapters or writing a rough draft.

Suggestions for Avoiding Distractions

1. *Close your door. Unplug your phone. Simply be unavailable.*

2. *Avoid the temptation to "finish one more errand," "make one more phone call," anything that takes up time you've already scheduled for studying.*

3. *Schedule your breaks and be specific about what you're going to do on your break. Just saying, "take a break" invites prolonged malingering.*

4. *Pile a whole bunch of junk on your bed so it's a real pain to try to get in it. Remember, we're trying to avoid temptation.*

5. *Identify people, places, and things that tend to tempt you and waste your time. Don't answer Carla's knock at your door. Don't go to the college cafeteria to study.*

6. *Get enough sleep. Eat right. Exercise.*

By the time Sara cleaned up the mess, got her drink, and got back to work, it was past 3:30. She decided to switch to working on math problems. About half an hour later, the doorbell rang. Sara grudgingly plodded downstairs, opened the door, and there stood her best friend Kim, jumping up and down, thrusting her hand under Sara's nose—she was wearing an engagement ring! Naturally, Sara had to hear every detail of the proposal, and the ring selection . . . and it was more than an hour later when Kim left.

Sara's 5:00 deadline had come and gone, and she still had not finished a single assignment. Now she had a choice to make: finish at least one assignment, skip her shower and not look as great as she'd hoped; or give up and try again tomorrow . . .

Obviously, Sara faced a lot of external distractions which sabotaged her studying plans. We think of distractions as "things" (or people) that tend to pull us off course, but there are also internal distractions that may plague us. For example, Sara faced that type of distraction when she was unable to maintain her concentration after the call from her date. Look at this list of possible distractions and see how many are best avoided simply by adjusting personal habits or attitudes:

1. Physical: hunger, thirst, fatigue, illness

2. Mental: daydreaming, personal problems, worrying, stress, thinking about other activities, or someplace you'd rather be

3. Environment: uncomfortable room/chair, wrong lighting, too hot or too cold, noise (phones, people, music, TV)

4. Other: negative attitude about assignment, course, or instructor; other people wanting your attention

The chart above offers some suggestions to avoid being distracted. You also have to plan ways to handle distractions when they occur and get yourself back on target.

Time Management Aids

There are many time management aids on the market today. They could be as simple as a calendar or a daily planner or as elaborate as an electronic organizer or a software program for a home computer. All of these tools can be very helpful to you for setting priorities, remembering important dates and deadlines and managing your life. If you don't already use one of these—start now. You can easily reduce your stress level if you let one of these time management aids do the remembering for you.

After you have developed your action plans which include deadlines, dates to remember and projected dates for completion, enter them into your organizer. The tool you use should include at least one month that can be viewed in its entirety. At a glance, a monthly or multi-week calendar helps you plan several days or weeks in advance. Doing this can help prevent important deadlines from "sneaking up" on you. Keep this calendar in a place where you know you will consult it often. If possible, make a copy of it and keep one with you at all times. Then, if new items need to be added, you can do so in one consistent place where you know the information will always be. When you return home, make it a point to transfer any new dates immediately. The small amount of time that it will take you to maintain a calendar will save you the enormous amount of stress caused by trying to remember all of the details that make up a busy life.

■ Summary

- It is important to identify personal, educational and career goals.
- By planning your time carefully, you will be able to better manage your educational, work and personal commitments.
- Develop strategies to deal with distractions and procrastination *before* they interrupt your study time.

Additional Resources

Resources in the Learning Resources Center (call numbers are shown in parentheses after the citation):

Carter, C. (1996). *Keys to success: how to achieve your goals.* Upper Saddle River, NJ: Prentice Hall. (LB2343.32 .C37 1996)

Jasper, J. (1999). *Take back your time: how to regain control of work, information, and technology.* New York: St. Martin's Griffin. (HD69 .T54 J37 1999)

Silber, L. T. (1998). *Time management for the creative person.* New York: Three Rivers Press. (HD69 .T54 S575 1998)

Web Sites:

Please note that web site addresses often change. If you are unable to reach the addresses below, use a search engine and search the source of the site or the title of the web document to find the new site.

Idaho State University, Time Management Study Tips:
http://www.isu.edu/departments/enroll/time.htm
John Townsend, Townsend International: http://www.stresstips.com/

On-Campus Resources:

Academic Skills Center, Center for the Technologies, Third Floor (401) 739-5000, Ext. 3416.

Activities

2-1   Complete the goal-setting worksheets located in the Appendix (pp. 166–167).

2-2   Read the Career Exploration sheet and generate five questions that you would like answered about your career.

■ Activity 2-2. Career Exploration

You have already begun making career decisions by deciding to come to New England Institute of Technology. Now is the time to question, explore and wonder about your technology and related career options. Listed below are some suggestions for researching your career. However, these are only suggestions. You need to identify **five questions** that you would like answered about your career. You may choose some of the questions listed below or write some of your own. Keep in mind that this is your opportunity to find out what YOU want to know about your career. When you have completed your research, write the answers to your career questions and include them in the Career Inventory Folder. These questions and answers should be neatly typed and free from grammatical and mechanical errors.

Suggestions for Career Research Activity

Use professional journals, newspapers, the Internet and World Wide Web to learn about the employment trends and career opportunities of your chosen employment area. Document where you obtained your research information.

Use the following questions as a guide and add any questions that are important to you.

- What kinds of duties, responsibilities and tasks do individuals in this career field do?
- Where are these people employed?
- What are the work conditions?
- What are the educational requirements?
- What is the employment outlook for this career field? What will the projected percent of growth of employers in this area be in five years? What will the percent of growth of employees in this area be in five years? What will the entry-level requirements in this area be in five years? What are some of the technological advancements expected in this area in five years?
- Do advancement opportunities exist?
- What are the advantages and disadvantages of this career field?
- What kinds of internships or co-op experiences should I seek to prepare me for work in this area?
- What are some of the opportunities for women in non-traditional careers?
- What are the opportunities for employment within a 100-mile radius? Would it be worthwhile to relocate?
- What are the varied personal and professional experiences an older worker can bring to a new career?

Suggestions for Career Research

■ Activity 2-2. Career Exploration Questions

Write your five career exploration questions below.

1. _____

2. _____

3. _____

4. _____

5. _____

CHAPTER 3
Connecting with Learning

"English is a second language for me, and because of this I found high school very difficult. New England Tech gave me the chance to prove to myself that I can accomplish any goal I set for myself. I received two honors during school, I was chosen as the "Best of Tech" for my technology and named to Who's Who Among Students In American Junior Colleges. Even more important, this school gave me the tools and confidence to take me closer to my goal of one day owning a design firm. My motto now is: Yes, I can do it!"

Emanuel Sousa
Interior Design Technology

Chapter Designers:

Mary L. Branco, Coordinator for High School Program
Doreen Lasiewski, Director of Instructional Development
Judith A. Nabb, Coordinator of Reading and Study Skills

What Students Are Saying . . .

"The presentation on understanding the learning process was one of the two best presentations we had. It enforced what I thought was my learning style but it also opened my eyes to other options that I need to look at. These other options could probably make me more efficient in all my learning experiences not just the ones at school."

Keith Maynard
Computer Information Systems Technology

In This Chapter

You will become familiar with and be able to describe the learning process and learning style theory.

You will learn how to

- Identify your learning style.
- Identify your learning needs.
- Use the Academic Skills Center (ASC).
- Set learning goals.

■ Introduction

Identifying your learning needs by understanding the learning process and recognizing how you learn best are an intricate part of your success as a college student and lifelong learner. This chapter will help you to do that and will give you the opportunity to explore and use the support services available at the Academic Skills Center (ASC). The ASC can assist you in assessing, developing and improving your reading, writing, math and study skills (academic skills).

The ASC provides a wide range of personalized services from individual tutoring to small group developmental and enrichment classes and study skills workshops. Some of the resources offered can also be accessed from your home if you own a computer with Internet access.

In this chapter, you will examine learning style theory, identify your learning style and learning needs and learn about multiple intelligences. You will explore ways in which the ASC can help you to strengthen and develop your skills. By the end of this chapter, you will have set specific learning goals.

■ Reading: Learning Styles/Instructional Styles

Introduction

The population at any college is a diverse one. Look around you at the composition of the students in your class. They come from all ages, ethnic, national, social, cultural, and religious backgrounds. Each person is indeed a unique individual. Each student has his/her own strengths and weaknesses along with his/her unique learning style. Each instructor you meet along the way will have a different teaching style. The people who will be guiding your educational experiences will also bring their personal attributes into the classroom. So what are you to do? How will you adapt to all of this diversity?

This chapter will focus on the differences in academic strengths, learning styles, and instructional styles. You will identify your strengths and learn how to compensate for your weaknesses. You will explore the many ways in which people receive information and determine the mode in which you learn best. Lastly, you will examine the different teaching techniques used in your classes and develop strategies to help you adapt your strengths, weaknesses, and learning styles to your instructors' teaching styles. These strategies will help you to be successful in college.

Strengths and Weaknesses

It is important to assess your strengths, especially in the areas of study skills and academics. You need to develop a sense of who you are, be confident about yourself, and know your strong suit. At the same time, you should become aware of the areas where you need improvement. If you are not realistic in this assessment, you may set yourself up for failure.

You have many strengths and are probably not aware of most of them. The following is an informal exercise that will focus on your strengths.

Strengths Exercise

Take a sheet of paper and print your name in large letters across the top of the page. Directly underneath your name print the word "STRENGTHS" in the same large letters. Then proceed to write down all of your strengths. Be sure to include everything good that you feel and think about yourself.

Are you a thoughtful person? A loyal friend? Are you a good cook? A guitar player? A winner at chess? Begin to think about your academic strengths. Are you good in Math? English? History? Computers? Now take your list and hang it in a place where you can look at it every day. Probably the best place to do this is on the mirror you use each morning. When you look into that mirror you will not only see yourself, but you will also see a list of your strengths. This "morale booster" will help you start the day with a positive, winning attitude.

Weaknesses Exercise

When you have completed your "strengths" list, continue to analyze yourself by making a "weaknesses" list. This time we have divided the page in half and have written the word "Weaknesses" in small letters in the left hand column. The right hand column is used to list strategies to compensate for your weaknesses.

Do you lose your temper easily? Are you always late for appointments and for classes? Do you have a difficult time in Math? Psychology? Science? Once again, begin to focus on your academic weaknesses. Use the following example to develop your list.

Here are some tips to use to accentuate your academic strengths:

1. **Be on time for class.** As we've said before, your instructor's perception of how serious a student you are plays a subtle, but important role in the subjective part of your grade. Straggling in late every day makes it look like this class is a low priority to you.

2. **Sit in the front of the class.** Most people tend to sit near the back, or at least in the "safe" middle seats. But, if you have the courage to sit up front, you will gain certain advantages. You can see the board and hear the instructor more clearly,

Example:

Weaknesses	Strategies
I am always late for class.	*I will set my alarm clock and get up 15 minutes earlier each day in order to be on time.*

which will help you take better notes. You won't be distracted by the antics of other students. You will usually get more attention and eye contact from the instructor, and it will be easier to ask questions.

3. **Pay attention in class.** Naturally your notes will be more complete if you are paying attention than if you are daydreaming. It also keeps you focused on the lecture or discussion, so later you can remember what was said in class. Many times students who don't pay attention complain that the stuff on the test was NEVER covered in class.

4. **Ask well thought out questions.** The more you participate, the more interesting the class becomes. If you are actively engaged in the learning process you will get more out of your classes, and they will be more enjoyable. Superficial questions and those that require only a yes/no answer don't help you probe the subject at a deeper level.

5. **Give your instructors positive feedback in class.** Your teachers will respond more readily to someone who is attentive, looks interested in learning, makes eye contact, nods his/her head in agreement, is willing to participate, and even smiles or laughs at the jokes. In other words, your teacher responds as any person would in a dialogue situation. You have no idea how difficult it is to teach a class of bored, sleepy looking students who never look up, never answer questions, stare blankly into space, or in other ways show that they wish they were somewhere else.

6. **Get to know fellow students.** This tip could improve your grade and your social life. Having someone to call for help with assignments, someone with whom you can compare notes and study for tests is a real asset. When you know the other people in your class, it makes discussions more interesting and less intimidating. Even a shy person can talk in front of friends. Should you ever have to miss a class, you can get the notes and find out what you missed from your classmates.

7. **Develop a support/study group.** This is an extension of the sixth point. Go beyond just knowing who else is in your class. Form a group that studies and works on difficult projects together. Some of you may have come from an educational system that emphasized competition rather than cooperation. You may be used to doing your schoolwork by yourself and may be reluctant to ask someone else for help. We now know, however, that people usually learn more as part of a group. In real life (and isn't school supposed to prepare you for real life?) you will get farther if you can work as part of a team that shares resources, information, and the workload.

8. **Develop your own learning tools.** Use your particular strengths to create study aids that will help you learn and remember information. Make charts, draw diagrams, construct models, record audio tapes, etc. In addition, gather the kinds of supplies and references you need to compensate for your academic weaknesses. If you are a poor speller, get a pocket sized dictionary or hand held spell checker to carry with you. If math computation is difficult, make sure you have a calculator. Study from your own textbooks so you can mark them to suit your needs.

9. **Complete all assignments on time.** Many instructors deduct points if an assignment is late. By turning your work in on time you give yourself the opportunity to earn the most points.

10. **Contact your instructor if you are going to be late or miss class.** If you are absent due to an emergency or critical illness, the instructor may let you turn in late work without penalty. Teachers are intelligent, but they are not mind readers—you have to let them know what's going on. They appreciate knowing their class is important to you, and that you are trying your best. On the other hand, don't bother calling in with flimsy excuses. I've had students ask me if it was OK to miss my class to go to _____. (You fill in the blank; I've heard them all!) As an adult you will set your own priorities, and they will probably be reflected in your grades.

11. **When overly burdened, seek support services.** Some students believe that asking for help or going for tutoring are signs of weakness. They think it is somehow "macho" or smart to "tough it out" on their own. Actually, the opposite is true. Getting help when you need it shows intelligence and resourcefulness.

To help you overcome your weaknesses, we have devoted several chapters of this book to topics that will assist you in developing your own strategies for success. Included among these are time management, improving your note taking, study and test taking skills, setting goals and developing action plans, building confidence with positive self-talk, and learning effective communication skills and relaxation techniques.

Learning Styles

Our brains do not all function in the same manner or on the same level. Not everyone learns in the same way. Your learning style is the way in which you gather, process, and retain information. It is both your preferred way of learning and the conditions under which you find it easiest to learn. In order to work to the best of your ability, it is important to discover your individual learning style. You can analyze your own style or use a standardized inventory.

One standardized instrument used in many counseling centers is the Myers-Briggs Personality Inventory. The Myers-Briggs provides information on your personality type, learning style and how you respond to work environments. It identifies four areas that include how you process information, how you receive information, how you make decisions, and how you prefer to carry out day to day activities. Each of these four scales shows two opposing preferences.

EXTROVERSION-INTROVERSION. This scale measures the extent to which you process information and focus your attention on the external environment or your internal world. For example, when you have a problem to solve, do you think of the best solution by talking about it with other people, or do you prefer to be alone and think it through by yourself? Are you more concerned with what is happening around you, or are you more focused on what you are thinking and feeling?

SENSING-INTUITION. This scale measures how you acquire information. Sensing refers to using your five senses (sight, smell, sound, touch, taste). Intuition is going by your sixth sense or gut feeling. Some people are famous for following through with their hunches; others, like Sgt. Joe Friday of *Dragnet* fame, want "just the facts, ma'am."

THINKING-FEELING. This scale measures how you make decisions. People who prefer the thinking mode make decisions by logically weighing out the pros and cons. The opposite side of the scale is making decisions based on values, emotions, and how the outcome will affect people. For example, when the Department of Transportation wants to build a new highway, should they take the shortest, easiest, most cost effective route? Or, should they worry about environmental concerns and people who will lose their family homes and have to be relocated?

JUDGING-PERCEIVING. This scale measures how you like to plan your day-to-day activities. Do you have your schedule set a week, month, or year in advance? Or, do you prefer to be spontaneous and leave your options open (in case you get a better offer)?

Why would you want to know this? The better you know yourself, the more you can capitalize on your natural strengths and preferences. If you know you learn better by processing externally, plan to study with a partner or group. If you like your schedule set, block off study and homework time well in advance. Knowing how you make decisions under stress can help you develop the best test taking strategies. Preferring to look at the big picture and being able to make intuitive leaps to a conclusion is very different than methodically following each step of a process. Which approach comes most naturally to you? There are times when you have to use each of the eight approaches. Some will come more easily and some will require you to make an extra effort.

In addition to your personality type, another component of your learning style is whether you are visually, auditorially, or kinesthetically oriented. To illustrate the three different kinds of learning styles, read the stories of the following four students: Victor Visual, Annie Auditory, Kenny Kinesthetic, and Terry Tactile.

Victor

Victor Visual learns best by seeing how things are done. He has always liked to read. Ever since he was little he was always aware of his surroundings. When he was a baby he liked to look at mobiles and the interesting toys his mother placed in his crib. His mom always said she could take him anywhere; he would sit there quietly, staring at the people and things around him. When he went to school Victor loved the brightly colored posters and bulletin board displays hanging on the walls of his classroom. He learned the ABCs by staring at the alphabet posted above the board. His teachers were impressed at his ability to recognize words at an early age. In fact, learning to read sight words was no problem for Victor.

In fourth grade when the class was studying planets, he suggested to the teacher that they hang models of the planets from the ceiling. He really did not want to construct the models, but he did make sure they were labeled correctly. In the sixth grade he qualified for the pizza party by reading more books than anyone else in his class. For his birthday, when he received toys that needed to be assembled, he always read the instructions before trying to put them together.

In high school Victor did well. He read his textbooks faithfully, but he really disliked classes where the teachers just lectured without using the board or providing handouts. When the teacher asked questions about the reading assignments from the night before, Victor was the only one who raised his hand, except for Vanessa Vision. At sixteen, when Victor learned to drive, he got 100% on the written test, but it took him three times to pass the behind-the-wheel portion of the test. Even now when Victor is going to drive somewhere he has never been before, he needs a good map with landmarks. In fact, Victor prefers written instructions for everything. In computer class Victor was one of the few students who actually read the manual.

As a college student Victor continues to do well in classes where the teacher uses the overhead projector or writes on the board. In lab classes he prefers that the instructor or another student do the experiments so he can watch. At home when Victor is watching TV, he becomes really annoyed when his younger brother stands in front of the TV. If he goes to an assembly or any kind of performance, he likes to sit in full view of the stage. He gets more out of the performance if he is able to see the speaker directly.

Annie

As a baby Annie Auditory could always be soothed with a lullaby. She liked to listen to her mother talk on the phone or with friends. Her favorite toy was a stuffed teddy bear that played music. She loved to have the radio or television turned on, and by the time she was three she had memorized all the commercials. She even knew the Empire Carpet phone number. She learned the alphabet by singing the ABC song. She learned her numbers in Spanish from hearing them sung on *SESAME STREET*.

In school Annie learned best by listening closely to the teacher. She needed to have everything explained. If the teacher did not read the directions at the top of the page, Annie had a hard time getting started on her seatwork. As she got older her teachers remarked how well Annie participated in class discussions. She always knew what was going on in school because she paid attention when the announcements were read over the loudspeaker. Annie's favorite birthday present was a cassette player/recorder. She loved to listen to books on tape, and has always liked listening to music. She also loved to record her own voice and play it back.

In high school Annie used the tape recorder to help her study. She made audio study guides and read her textbook onto a tape so she could listen to it again. She understood the chapters better if she could hear them. She enjoyed getting her friends together to study for an exam by discussing the material for the test. She became proficient in foreign language classes because she was able to pick up the inflections and the accents. When Annie started to drive, her instructor usually had to tell her where to turn and when to stop. Even now when Annie gets lost, she needs to stop and ask someone to tell her the directions. Giving her a map would not do her any good.

Annie enjoys lecture classes in college; she hates long reading assignments. She did well in Music Appreciation, but had difficulty with her Introduction to the Visual Arts course. If it were not for the Visual Arts course, Annie would have a 4.0 GPA. In fact, Annie has considered becoming a college instructor because she likes to talk and conduct class discussions.

Kenny and Terry

Kenny Kinesthetic and Terry Tactile are best friends. They have been together since their sandbox days. In the sandbox they built roads, houses, and elaborate castles. As babies they always had to have something in their hands. They clung to their bottles and pacifiers long after other kids had given them up; but, as his mom liked to point out, Kenny was walking by eight months. The boys both learned the alphabet by playing with blocks.

In grammar school they loved working with play dough and messy art projects. Learning to read was a little more difficult for Kenny and Terry. They fidgeted if too much time was spent doing seatwork. If they really needed to concentrate it helped to be able to color, cut and paste, or at least drum a pencil on the desk. The teachers thought they were hyperactive and always told them to sit still. They spent a lot of time in the hall.

When Victor suggested making models of the planets, Kenny and Terry were the first to volunteer to do the job. They got into those science experiments in junior high and for the first time felt good about learning.

In high school they were chemistry lab partners who always got an A on their experiments (except when they blew up the lab because they just had to see what happened when they mixed the pink stuff with the green stuff). Shop classes were their specialty. Their mothers had more knick-knacks, spice racks, and towel holders than any other moms in the PTA. Kenny and Terry had a flair for fixing things, and never had to read the directions to assemble anything. They learned to drive one day by taking Terry's father's car to an empty parking lot while he was taking his Sunday afternoon nap. They both had to take the written test over, though, before they actually got their licenses. It's a good thing PE counts as a high school requirement. They really needed those credits to graduate.

At college both Kenny and Terry do well in lab classes, technical courses, and art courses where there is not too much written work. In English they never read a book if there is a movie version available. They signed up for the fitness center immediately and will probably try out for sports. These two guys are pretty much alike. Terry is better at hand/eye coordination and working with his hands, while Kenny is better in athletics and physical activities.

The Three Basic Learning Styles

From our stories about Victor, Annie, Kenny and Terry we have illustrated some of the strengths of three distinct learning styles: visual, auditory and kinesthetic/tactile. Visual learners use their eyesight, or vision, as their preferred method of taking in information and learn best by reading or watching a demonstration. Auditory learners use their ears or sense of hearing the most. They prefer to learn by listening to a lecture, discussion, or audio tape. Kinesthetic/tactile learners are much better at getting information by using their sense of touch. They prefer to learn by doing or becoming physically involved with what they are studying. If they do have to read or listen, it helps if they can move around or do something with their hands.

These Learning Styles reflect preferences in the way we learn. Knowing that you are a visual learner doesn't mean that you don't understand what you hear. It means that given a choice, you would usually prefer to read or watch. Visual learners usually fare quite well in grade school, where teachers cater to this style. Go into any preschool through fifth grade classroom, and you will be bombarded with visual stimulation. Elementary school teachers all learn how to create effective bulletin board displays. They want to make sure that any kid who is not paying attention is still learning something while he/she stares at the walls, ceiling, windows, or even out the door into the hall. Since reading plays such an important role in education, visual learners who like to read seem to

Visual learners learn best by:

| Reading | Watching demonstrations | Seeing pictures |

Strategies for visual learners include:

Printed materials	Movies	Blackboard demonstrations
Diagrams	Charts	Photos
Graphs	Handouts	Illustrations
Reading textbook before lecture	Taking notes to read after lecture	Overheads/transparencies

Auditory learners learn best by:

| Listening | Conversation |
| Asking questions | Discussing |

Strategies for auditory learners include:

Study groups	Study buddy	Audio tapes
Movies	Recitation	
Reading textbook following lecture		

Tactile/Kinesthetic learners learn best by:

| Doing | Touching |
| Moving | Feeling |

Strategies for tactile/kinesthetic learners include:

Hands on learning	Experiments	Interactive learning
Teamwork	Role playing	Workshops
Performance models	Note taking (writing out what you see or hear)	Collecting samples
Becoming physically involved		

Concentrating on how the reading and the listening will benefit you in experimentation.

do well, even in high school. They will do well in college if they can take good notes. They should try to get everything important written into their notes to read and look at when studying for a test.

Auditory learners, on the other hand, may find college classes more to their liking because many instructors use the lecture/discussion method of teaching. In the lower grades auditory learners can get bored with too much seatwork and reading. On the whole, though, they probably did fine in school since most teachers at that level explain everything in detail. As they get older, their auditory strengths are used even more as verbal reasoning skills are emphasized.

Tactile and kinesthetic styles vary slightly. Tactile learners like to use their hands, while kinesthetic learners use their whole body whenever possible. These two styles are so similar, though, that throughout this chapter we will use the terms synonymously. These learners are probably the least understood in schools. Although some teachers really try to bring in hands-on approaches to learning, others find it difficult to adapt their more audio/visual styles to a kinesthetic child. Because that child usually needs to be moving around while taking in the information, the typical classroom arrangement makes school more difficult. Not surprisingly, most of the developmental students in my college classes discover that they are kinesthetic/tactile learners. They never quite "got it" in grade school and high school because they were never given the opportunity to learn most subjects in their preferred style.

So that brings us to the here and now. Perhaps you could see yourself in the stories of Victor, Annie, Kenny, or Terry. You're saying "That's me! That's the way I learn best." It's great to know your strengths so you can use them to your best advantage. But since life is not always fair, and your instructors will not always teach in your preferred style, you need to learn some strategies to compensate for the other styles that are less developed in you.

Student Environment

The environment around you is another factor that influences your learning. The time of day when people participate in an activity often will determine how well or how poorly they perform. Students who take courses or study at the times when they are most alert tend to do better. (Don't you wonder how many research studies it took to verify that amazing fact?!) Still, many people do not even consider this when they schedule their classes or plan their study time. Are you a morning person or a night person? Do you peak mid-morning or fizzle in the middle of the afternoon? If you can't keep your eyes open after 9:00 p.m., don't plan to study for your chemistry test after the rest of the family has gone to bed.

The surrounding environment will also have an effect on how you perform. Do you prefer a room that is loud vs. one that is quiet? Must you work on a neat desk, or does it matter whether or not it is cluttered? What about the lighting? Or the room temperature? What is it that makes you comfortable? It is very difficult to concentrate when you are uncomfortable. If the room is too cold, your mind may concentrate more on keeping warm than on your algebra problems.

Instructional Styles

Three types of instructional styles most often used by teachers are independent, student centered, and cooperative learning. The first is very formal and businesslike. The instructor delivers his/her class material primarily by lecturing, and the student has no input into the class lecture. The student is almost totally responsible for learning independently. S/he is expected to take notes, follow the syllabus, read the textbook, complete the assignments, and prepare for assorted quizzes and exams. This type of learning places the importance on the individual student's efforts and usually takes place in classes with large enrollments.

The second type of instructional style is less formal. Discussion is introduced into the classroom along with the lecture. The instructor attempts to involve the group into the learning process by asking probing questions that encourage students to think, answer questions and make comments. The lecture delivery is in a traditional format, but the instructor requires class participation by calling on students, if necessary.

Study Strategies for the Three Learning Modes

Visual Learner	Auditory Learner	Kinesthetic Learner

Visual Learner

Note Taking

1. Sit in the front of the room
2. Sit away from any windows
3. Ask for graphs & charts to help you remember main concepts.
4. Request written instructions.
5. Reword notes into charts & graphs.
6. Draw pictures of important topics in your notes.
7. Try mapping your notes.

Reading

1. Survey text by looking at visual aids (pictures, graphs, & charts) before you start to read.
2. As you read make a visual map of key headings and concepts.
3. Make charts and schematics of difficult concepts.
4. Create study note cards for terminology and formulae.
5. Use 2, 3, or 4 color highlighting system-one color for main points, another for examples, a third for terminology, etc.

Exam Preparation

1. Use visual images to remember main points.
2. Use flash cards.
3. Check library for films and visual aids pertaining to your subject matter.

Test taking

1. Request written instructions if none are provided.
2. Draw charts, maps, etc. to help you recall information.

Auditory Learner

Note Taking

1. Try rhyming your notes.
2. Sit close to the speaker.
3. Repeat important quotes quietly.
4. Listen for specific information-- don't let note taking interfere with listening.
5. Use a tape recorder when appropriate. Listen to the tape and update notes as soon as possible after each class.
6. Participate in class discussion.

Reading

1. Survey by reading chapter headings and asking survey questions out loud.
2. Try reading difficult sections out loud.
3. Summarize out loud immediately after reading a paragraph or section.
4. Listen to books on tape.

Exam Preparation

1. Read important notes or reading material out loud.
2. Record and listen to vocabulary for each day's lesson.
3. Talk about what you've learned. Participate in study groups or just tell a friend (or teach yourself.)
4. Tape yourself reading or reciting things you need to remember.
5. Try rhyming-make poems and rhymes to help you remember facts etc.

Test taking

1. Listen for verbal instructions.
2. Repeat instructions quietly to yourself.

Kinesthetic Learner

Note Taking

1. Keep moving--move during lecture as much as the situation allows.
2. Raise your hand and volunteer to answer questions frequently.
3. Take copious notes
4. Recopy notes or type on a computer.
5. Participate in class discussions.
6. Build or draw what you're learning about.

Reading

1. Survey by writing preview questions and answers. Write as you review.
2. Use workbooks and computers whenever possible.
3. Try to write a summary after reading a difficult paragraph or section.
4. Take notes on your reading in the margins of the text or in a notebook.

Exam Preparation

1. Participate in labs, discussions, field work, etc.
2. Use the equipment, tools, models, etc, of a subject area as frequently as possible.
3. Seek on-the-job training, work-study, field-work, lab work, etc., that allows you to become physically involved in your area of study
4. Exercise while studying-run in place, walk, stretch, etc.
5. Build or draw what you're learning about.
6. Use rhythm to remember.

Test taking

1. Position yourself so that you have plenty of room to move.
2. To aid recall in an exam, try moving in your chair and/or feel yourself doing a procedure.

The third type of instructional style makes a concerted effort to involve the students in group dynamics. Not only are lectures peppered with question and answer sessions, but students may be involved in lab work, demonstrations, presentations, and/or group problem-solving exercises. In some cases the teacher does not lecture at all, and the students are totally responsible for discovering the information on their own. The instructor serves as a facilitator and resource person. In cooperative learning the students work as teams and may even do their exams together.

When it is impossible for you to find an instructor with a compatible teaching style, make an honest effort to learn. Sit in the front of the classroom to be certain that you do not miss anything. Not only should you listen to what your instructor is saying, but you need to watch for facial expressions and body language. Note where emphasis is placed during a discussion or lecture, pay close attention to board work and/or overhead transparencies used in class, and be aware of the material that will be covered in class. You can always do this by reading your textbook before each class.

Study for the class in your best learning style mode. Rewrite or tape your notes. Read your notes or textbook out loud. Do whatever it takes to learn. Talk with the instructor if you have problems; ask questions when you do not understand. Seek out available tutorial services to provide that extra edge.

■ Multiple Intelligences

Learning styles describe how we prefer to take in and process new information. Intelligence is somewhat different. According to one theory, intelligence is ". . . the ability to respond successfully to new situations and the capacity to learn from one's past experiences" (Armstrong, p. 8). Many people commonly think of intelligence as the kind of inborn learning ability that is measured with one of the many types of IQ (intelligence quotient) tests administered regularly in schools. In fact, research indicates that, though IQ tests are a good predictor of school success, they do not predict "real world" success. In one study, Armstrong cites that one-third of a group of highly successful professional people had low IQ scores.

Some theorists believe that we've focused too much attention on verbal and logical thinking, neglecting other ways of knowing. For example, if your computer crashed, who would be the best person to seek for assistance? Would you go to your English instructor or a student in the Computer and Network Servicing program? Intelligence depends on the context, task and what information is needed in a particular situation.

Howard Gardner's theory of Multiple Intelligences proposes that there are many kinds of intelligences. His theory recognizes the intelligence of the athlete, mechanic, architect, counselor and teacher as different but equally valid. Based on research taken from many types of physical and psychological studies, Gardner's theory has been recognized for about 20 years. The eight intelligences are:

- ■ linguistic—the ability to use oral and written language easily
- ■ logical-mathematical—the ability to solve problems using abstract reasoning, mathematical ability and logic
- ■ spatial—the ability to mentally comprehend shapes and three-dimensional images
- ■ musical—the ability to perceive and comprehend rhythm, pitch and melody
- ■ bodily-kinesthetic—the ability to use the body with control, agility, balance and grace
- ■ interpersonal—the ability to perceive the emotions and motivations of others

(8) Multiple Intelligences

INTELLIGENCE	DESCRIPTION	NEIT	FAMOUS PERSON
LINGUISTIC	WORD SMART ARGUE ENTERTAIN PERSUADE INSTRUCT READ & WRITE WELL GOOD JEOPARDY CONTESTANT	CBM, VRP,HUS.S., EN 102, Oral Communications, ASC, LRC	
Logical Mathematical	NUMBERS SMART RATIONAL OUTLOOK LOOK FOR CAUSE & EFFECT	CST, CIS, ELS, Math Dept., MA110, 120, 210, STATISTICS, Financial Aid, ASC	
SPATIAL	THINK IN PICTURES & IMAGES DRAW & SKETCH (3) DIMENSIONALLY ORIENTED	ID, ABTA, ADBT, CC, MDME, META	
MUSICAL	PRODUCE, PERCEIVE, APPRECIATE RHYTHMS & MELODIES "GOOD EAR" SING	HISTORY OF ROCK & ROLL CULTURES OF MUSIC	
BODILY KINESTHETIC	INTELLIGENCE OF PHYSICAL SELF TACTILE FREQUENT BODY MOVEMENT ENJOY SEWING, HIKING, CAMPING, MODEL BUILDING	OTA, ST, MT, CC, PLBH, RACH, AUT, AUTB, NEIT golf team	
INTERPERSONAL	WORK WITH OTHERS PERCEIVE & RESPOND TO MOODS, TEMPERAMENTS, DESIRES, INTENTIONS OF OTHERS	OFFICE OF STUDENT SUPPORT SERVICES, CAREER SERVICES	
INTRAPERSONAL	INTELLIGENCE OF INNER SELF INTROSPECTIVE, SOUL SEARCHER -OR- HIGHLY GOAL-ORIENTED INDEPENDENT SELF-DISCIPLINED	YOUR SA, BUSINESS MANAGEMENT TECH	
NATURALIST	EXPERTISE IN CLASSIFICATION OF SPECIES "GREEN THUMB" INTELLIGENCE FOR ANIMALS	AMA, MT, ST	
EXISTENTIAL (PENDING)	CONCERN WITH ULTIMATE LIFE ISSUES- WHAT IS LIFE? WHAT IS THIS ALL ABOUT? DOES GOD EXIST?	WORLD RELIGIONS, ETHICS & HUMAN VALUES	

Assessing My Multiple Intelligences

INSTRUCTIONS: Complete each sentence below by filling in the blank with the number that best indicates your skill level in each. Enter the number in the blank before the statement. Total the score for each intelligence in the box at the bottom of the column.

4	3	2	1	0
exceptional	high	moderate	minimal	none

Verbal/Linguistic

- I read and understand what I've read with—
- I listen to the radio or a spoken-word cassette and understand with—
- I play word games like Scrabble, Anagrams, or Password with—
- I make up tongue twisters, nonsense rhymes, or puns with—
- I use words in writing or speaking with—
- In my English, social studies, and history courses in school, I displayed—
- Others have recognized that my writing shows—
- I often convince others to agree with me with—
- I speak in public with—
- I use words to create mental pictures with—

Total ☐

Logical/Mathematical $2A(B)=C^2$

- I compute numbers in my head with—
- In my math and/or science courses in school, I displayed—
- I play games or solve brainteasers that require logical thinking with—
- I identify regularities or logical sequences in things with—
- I think in clear, abstract concepts with—
- I find logical flaws in things that people say and do with—
- I categorize and analyze information with—
- I piece together patterns from separate pieces of information with—
- I use symbols to manipulate data with—
- Others have recognized that my deductive ability shows—

Total ☐

Visual/Spatial

- I am able to use color with—
- I use a camera or camcorder to record what I see around me with—
- I do jigsaw puzzles, mazes, and other visual puzzles with—
- I format and layout publications with—
- I find my way around unfamiliar territory with—
- I draw or paint with—
- In Geometry classes in school, I displayed—
- I understand what a shape will look like when viewing it from directly above with—
- I design interior or exterior spaces with—
- I recognize shapes regardless of the angle from which I view them with—

Total ☐

Bodily/Kinesthetic

- I play tennis, golf, swim, or engage in some similar physical activity with—
- I sew, weave, or engage in some similar creative activity with—
- I build models, do woodworking, or construct things with—
- In activities or courses requiring physical or manual dexterity in school, I display—
- I use gestures or other forms of body language to convey ideas with—
- My physical coordination displays—
- I dance with—
- I express my feelings through physical activity with—
- I am recognized as having physical or manual abilities that exhibit—
- My dramatic ability shows—

Total ☐

Continued on back

© 1995 National Dropout Prevention Center at Clemson University
205 Martin Street, Clemson, SC 29634-0726 (864) 656-2599

Assessing My Multiple Intelligences

INSTRUCTIONS: Complete each sentence below by filling in the blank with the number that best indicates your skill level in each. Enter the number in the blank before the statement. Total the score for each intelligence in the box at the bottom of the column.

4	3	2	1	0
exceptional	high	moderate	minimal	none

Musical

- __ I sing with—
- __ I can tell when a musical note is off-key with—
- __ I can sight read and sing or play a difficult musical piece with—
- __ I play a musical instrument with—
- __ I can hear a melody once and reproduce it with—
- __ I reproduce or create intricate rhythms with—
- __ I create new musical compositions with—
- __ I am recognized by others as having musical talent with—
- __ I direct others in creating musical selections with—
- __ I "hear" the patterns of relationships within a musical piece with—

Total [ ]

Interpersonal

- __ I provide advice or counsel to others with—
- __ My ability to facilitate group work shows—
- __ I make friends with—
- __ I play social games such as Pictionary or Charades with—
- __ When teaching another person or groups of people, I display—
- __ In leading others, I exhibit—
- __ My involvement in social activities connected with my work, church, or community displays—
- __ I am able to understand the needs and emotions of others with—
- __ I work together with others to achieve a common goal with—
- __ I sense other people's motives or hidden agendas with—

Total [ ]

Intrapersonal/ Introspective

- __ I reflect on ideas or events with—
- __ I achieve personal growth by using new information with—
- __ I achieve a resilience to setbacks with—
- __ I have developed a special hobby or interest with—
- __ I set important goals for my life with—
- __ I recognize my strengths and weaknesses (borne out by feedback from other sources) with—
- __ I use solitude to strengthen my inner resources with—
- __ I am strong willed or independent minded to a degree that exhibits—
- __ I keep a personal diary or journal to record the events of my inner life in a way that displays—
- __ I seek to understand my own motivation with—

Total [ ]

Naturalist

- __ I can see variations in leaves with—
- __ I am able to identify a wide variety of insects, birds, or rocks with—
- __ Using a microscope, I can see very small differences between plants or animals with—
- __ I can identify the tracks and spoors of an animal with—
- __ I am able to tell the difference between harmless and poisonous plants or animals with—
- __ Using a telescope, I am able to identify stars, planets, and galaxies with—
- __ I can plan an attractive garden that has color during all four seasons of the year with—
- __ I am able to work with animals with—
- __ I am able to classify such things as rocks or aquatic life or clouds with—
- __ I am able to grow plants with—

Total [ ]

© 1995 National Dropout Prevention Center at Clemson University
205 Martin Street, Clemson, SC 29634-0726 (864) 656-2599

■ intrapersonal—the ability to perceive the inner emotions and motivations of oneself

■ naturalist—the ability to identify and classify patterns in nature

Gardner (1993) states "it becomes important to consider individuals as a collection of aptitudes rather than as having a singular problem-solving faculty that can be measured directly through pencil-and-paper tests" (p. 27). Though very few people have highly developed forms of all eight intelligences, most people possess a collection of various degrees of each intelligence. By recognizing which intelligences are your most developed and which are weakest, you can begin to maximize and celebrate your strengths and learn ways to overcome or minimize your weaknesses.

■ Using the Academic Skills Center (ASC)

The Academic Skills Center (ASC) provides a wide variety of services on campus and on their web site that can help you discover your learning style and help you to develop good study strategies. In the ASC, you can brush up on your learning skills if you've been out of school for a while, learn some study skills, improve your reading, speaking, writing and listening skills. Some of these skills are taught in developmental and enrichment classes and in workshops, others are available through one-on-one tutoring. Stop in and see how the helpful staff at the ASC can help you to become a better learner.

What's Available at the Academic Skills Center's Web Site?

■ *under READING, you'll find strategies for improving your reading, with links to other sites with helpful information*

■ *under WRITING, you'll find information on writing a summary and an example of a term paper in APA (American Psychological Association) format*

■ *under STUDY SKILLS, you'll find a number of other interesting links that provide valuable information on these topics:*

   ■ *time management—some quick tips on managing your time*

   ■ *learning goals—information on forming and establishing Learning Goals*

   ■ *note taking—links to sites related to taking notes efficiently and studying from those notes*

   ■ *test tips—effective strategies to prepare for and take tests*

   ■ *learning styles—links to in-depth information about learning styles, web sites on developing your intelligences, about Howard Gardner and his theory of multiple intelligences as well as an online learning style inventory*

   ■ *reflective worksheet—a worksheet to help you summarize what you learned in this chapter and at the ASC web site*

On the ASC web site, you can learn more about learning styles by following links to a number of different sites. Clicking on the Reading/Writing/Study skills button leads you to a number of choices tailored to your interests and abilities. Exploring the links at this web site can supply you with interesting information, enjoyable and enlightening self-tests and useful tips and strategies to improve the way you learn. Whether in person or online, the Academic Skills Center is available to help.

■ Setting Learning Goals

In the previous chapter, you learned about setting career and educational goals. In this section, we'll get more specific about educational or learning goals. First, what is a learning goal? A learning goal provides a road map to becoming the best student possible. You may need to set a short-term goal to pass a quiz or a long-term goal to graduate with honors. A learning goal gives you direction. Even if you don't achieve all of your learning goals, you will have gained invaluable tools along the way which will help you to be a strong, effective student.

 earning goals help to guide you toward the direction you have carefully chosen.

Reasons for Having Learning Goals

- Learning goals provide you with direction in your studies.
- Any goal gives you a sense of accomplishment when you have achieved it.
- Learning goals can help motivate you to tackle difficult learning situations.
- Learning goals give you a way to evaluate yourself.
- Learning goals help you to structure your time.
- Accomplished learning goals make you look good—both to yourself and to others.
- Learning goals contribute to your sense of confidence as a learner.

How Do I Set a Learning Goal?

Any goal should be conceivable, believable, desirable, achievable and measurable.

- Conceivable—can you picture it?
- Believable—can it happen?
- Desirable—do you want to achieve it?
- Achievable—is it realistic?
- Measurable—can you set a standard for accomplishing it?

The first step to setting a learning goal is to identify your learning needs. You may determine that you are not as organized as you would like to be, which makes it difficult to get assignments done on time. Maybe you have some difficulty reading technical materials or taking notes. Whatever learning weakness you may have, there are resources available on campus to help you set goals and devise strategies to strengthen your skills and become a better learner.

Some Examples of Learning Goals:

The following examples illustrate how two students at New England Tech identified their learning needs and set learning goals to develop the skills that they needed to perform more effectively.

Example One: Tony, a Multimedia Technology student, recognized that writing for his English 101 class was a real challenge for him. He labored for hours over a one-paragraph summary. Tony knew that he didn't have a lot of experience with writing and, therefore, lacked the confidence and skill to feel comfortable with his writing. He recognized that he needs good writing skills to make it in his technology and beyond. Determined to improve his skills, he visited the ASC and met with a skills specialist. Tony shared his frustrations about writing with the skills specialist. He also indicated that he is a visual learner (like many students in his technology) and loves to work on the computer. Tony dedicated the five-week intersession period to working on improving his writing skills. Before he started his English 102 class in the July quarter, he planned on spending two sessions per week at the ASC, working through a writing software package with the guidance of a skills specialist. The software package led him through the writing process, giving ample opportunity to write several different types of essays. The skills specialist then gave him feedback on each essay. Ultimately, Tony knew that his hard work paid off when he entered English 102 feeling and acting like a confident writer.

You can become a more successful learner by identifying your learning needs and improving your skills early in your course work.

In this example, Tony has the very specific goal of improving his writing skills. Using the goal-setting techniques from this chapter, he set a goal that is conceivable, believable, desirable, achievable and measurable. By using the goal-setting techniques described in Chapter Two, he chose a specific goal (to improve his writing) and identified multiple actions or strategies to accomplish that goal (meeting with a skills specialist, working through the software package). Tony also decided how he would work through each action/strategy (complete writing exercises and get feedback on each essay) and when he expected to accomplish his goal (during the intersession). This example shows how some careful planning and focused effort can help a student overcome an obstacle to better grades early in his college career so that he can perform more successfully in the rest of his classes.

Example Two: During his first quarter at New England Tech, Jonathan, an Internet Communications Technology student, felt that he barely made it through the quarter after completing two major projects following a series of sleepless nights. He was tired of doing things at the last minute and trying to keep everything he had to get done in his head all the time. Jonathan finally decided to do something about his procrastination problem and took a one-credit time management course at the Academic Skills Center. After taking the course, Jonathan was better able to manage his workload (and stress level) by planning ahead and allowing ample time to complete work before deadlines crept up on him.

In Jonathan's case, the problem wasn't with his academic skills, but with self-management. After recognizing his weakness, he set a goal of dealing with his tendency to procrastinate. Jonathan took advantage of a time management workshop to get some valuable tips on how to better plan his time. He set a realistic and achievable goal by using the College's resources to improve his performance. Jonathan is now better able to manage his workload and his stress level by completing assignments on time.

In both cases, the students identified obstacles to peak performance and set goals designed to help them work more efficiently. They made a conscious choice to succeed as students by addressing their difficulties early in their college careers and by taking advantage of the services provided to help them improve. After accomplishing their goals, they were better able to meet the demands of their classes.

■ Summary

- ■ We all learn differently and develop preferred ways of processing information.
- ■ Howard Gardner's theory of multiple intelligences identifies eight kinds of "intelligence" that are not measured the way that the traditional notion of intelligence is measured. Those intelligences are: linguistic, logical-mathematical, spatial, musical, bodily-kinesthetic, interpersonal, intrapersonal and naturalist.
- ■ Identifying your learning style and your developed intelligences can help you to select learning strategies that work best for you.
- ■ Capitalize on your strengths and develop your academic skills by setting specific learning goals and using the resources at the ASC.

Additional Resources

Resources in the Learning Resources Center (call numbers are shown in parentheses after the citation):

Hansen, R. S. (1997). *Write your way to a higher GPA: how to dramatically boost your GPA simply by sharpening your writing skills.* Berkeley, CA: Ten Speed Press. (PE1408 .H329 1997)

Linksman, R. (1996). *How to learn anything quickly: an accelerated program for rapid learning.* Secaucus, NJ: Carol Publishing Group. (LB1060 .L535 1996)

Roberts, J. M. (1999). *Effective study skills: maximizing your academic potential.* Upper Saddle River, NJ: Prentice Hall. (LB2395 .R63 1999)

Web Sites:

Please note that web site addresses often change. If you are unable to reach the addresses below, use a search engine and search the source of the site or the title of the web document to find the new site.

Learning Styles
The Learning Web: http://www.thelearningweb.net
Telecommunications for Remote Work and Learning:
    http://granite.cyg.net/%7Ejblackmo/diglib/styl.html
Penn State Center for Learning and Academic Technologies,
    General Education Modules (GEMs), Learning Style Inventory:
    http://www.clat.psu.edu/gems/Other/LSI/LSI.htm

Multiple Intelligences/Howard Gardner
CIO.com: The Leading Resource for Information Executives:
    http://www.cio.com/archive/031596_qa.html
SouthWestern Opportunities Network:
    http://www.swopnet.com/ed/TAG/7_Intelligences.html
American Education Network Corporation:
    http://www.aenc.org/SiteOverview- Multi-Int-FS.html

On-Campus Resources:

Academic Skills Center, Center for the Technologies, Third Floor (401) 739-5000, Ext. 3416.

Activities

3-1 Access the ASC web page and investigate the reading, writing and study skills links, where you will receive helpful information and materials. There will also be links to information available at other learning centers, including a link to a Learning Styles Inventory. Materials on setting learning goals are found by clicking on the study skills button.

-OR-

If you have already attended a Study Skills Workshop the week before classes began, complete the reflective worksheet. Then, go to the section on setting learning goals by clicking on the study skills button on the ASC Web page to get the information that you need to complete the worksheet on setting learning goals.

3-2 Based on the results of your tour, complete a reflective worksheet in which you identify your learning needs and the areas of the ASC that will help you to develop the skills that you need to be a successful learner. This worksheet will help you to complete your self-assessment that is required at the end of this course.

3-3 Complete the worksheet on setting learning goals that will help you target specific learning goals.

■ Activity 3-2. Reflective Worksheet

1. What did you learn about yourself in respect to your learning style(s) after taking the Learning Style Inventory linked to the ASC web page?

————————————————————————————————————

————————————————————————————————————

————————————————————————————————————

————————————————————————————————————

————————————————————————————————————

2. What are your strengths in terms of multiple intelligences? What intelligences would you like to develop?

————————————————————————————————————

————————————————————————————————————

————————————————————————————————————

————————————————————————————————————

————————————————————————————————————

3. What did you learn about the Academic Skills Center (ASC) after touring its web site?

————————————————————————————————————

————————————————————————————————————

————————————————————————————————————

————————————————————————————————————

4. What specific areas of the ASC will you utilize to help you to develop the skills you need to be successful in college?

————————————————————————————————————

————————————————————————————————————

————————————————————————————————————

————————————————————————————————————

■ Activity 3-3. Applying the Steps for Setting Learning Goals

This exercise will give you the opportunity to utilize some of what you have found out about yourself as a learner in order to set a realistic learning goal.

1. Name a specific, clear, conceivable learning goal.

   _____

   _____

2. Based on the information you have discovered about yourself as a learner, is your goal believable? Can it happen and why?

   _____

   _____

   _____

   _____

3. What makes attaining this goal desirable? What motivates you? Be specific.

   _____

   _____

   _____

   _____

4. In order to determine if it is achievable, identify the individual steps that need to be done to complete the goal.

   _____

   _____

   _____

   _____

5. How will you know you've attained your goal? What will be your reward?

   _____

   _____

   _____

   _____

CHAPTER 4
Taking Control of Your Life

"When I make a commitment to a specific goal, I have to do my absolute best to achieve it. My decision to pursue an education meant making some sacrifices. I have tried to teach my children that the best and most satisfying things in life are the ones you work hard for. I worked very hard at NEIT and graduated with a 4.0 GPA. I was really happy to be the recipient of the Best of Tech and Tech Scholar awards. I will continue to work hard in my position as a surgical technologist at Day Kimball Hospital."

Leah Cantelmo
Surgical Technology

Chapter Designers:

Steven S. Calabro, Director of Counseling Services
Lee Peebles, Director of Student Advising

What Students Are Saying . . .

"Taking control of my future and of my education has to be done by me not anyone else. Being able to control one's life is something that will not just benefit me while I attend NEIT. It will benefit me throughout my career and life. Knowing that I can depend on myself to get the job done when it needs to be is a skill that many employers look for. This quarter of TEC 101 was a good wake up call for me to realize that in order for me to succeed in this technology and in the future I have to want to do it myself and not rely on others."

Fabio Ferreira
Electronics Technology

In This Chapter

You will learn how to:

- Recognize, develop and exercise personal management skills.
- Describe the personal management skills necessary to become an effective independent learner.

◾ Introduction

As a college student, taking control of your life requires a set of skills that can assist you in meeting your personal and career goals. One important feature of taking control is to accept ownership, responsibility and accountability for the life that is yours, a process referred to as self-management. It is important to view yourself as having influence over the events that occur in your life. One inescapable feature of life is change; how you view that change will determine how well you are able to cope. Change can be stressful and stress requires management skill. The recommended ways of managing your stress level are learning how to say "No," maintaining balance, coping and understanding what you can control. Another way of controlling your stress is to effectively manage your time and set priorities. Building a system of support can help you meet all of the demands discussed above. The final ingredient to the recipe of personal success is developing and maintaining motivation. This chapter will provide you with an understanding of the skills necessary to take effective control of your life.

◾ Coping with Change

We live in a dynamic world where change is inevitable. The degree to which you are successful at meeting the challenges of change will be determined by how effective you are at coping. While you may not be able to control whether or not change occurs, you are able to determine your response to change. Change provides the opportunity to know that which was previously unknown. For some, this can be a frightening prospect. However, when viewed from a different perspective, it can be a stepping stone to growth. Individuals who experience difficulty at adapting to change do so because of a fear of the unknown. This fear causes individuals to avoid a situation instead of seeing a new situation as a resource for learning. The key is to view

See change as an opportunity for growth rather than a situation to be avoided.

the change as an opportunity for growth rather than a situation to be avoided. Remember—life is a matter of choice. Choose well and enjoy the benefits of good decision-making when coping with change.

■ Relax and Keep Perspective

Stress is defined as a physiological and/or psychological demand placed upon a person. Your capacity to respond to that demand will determine the degree to which you are affected. You can determine how you are affected by the value you assign to the stressor (person, place or thing). If you value an event with a high degree of importance, you are more likely to become stressed. Conversely, if you value an event to a lesser degree, you are less likely to be stressed. This clearly places *you* in control of your own stress.

The ability to maintain balance in your life will have a significant impact on whether or not you become stress-managed. The state of balance presumes that you are centered in your thinking, feelings and action. Life will continue to present you with an endless stream of challenges each day that you awaken. Your ability to maintain balance will affect your ability to maintain a reasonable perspective. This information will assist you in your decision-making as it relates to stress. The next reading includes strategies designed to assist you in managing your stress.

■ Reading: When the Going Gets Tough

Reflect for a minute on the issues you'll be facing in the 21st Century: ongoing, and rapid change, information overload, dealing with people unlike yourself, uncharted career paths, and enormous societal problems. Every one of these phenomena can be stressful, but change—rapid, constant change—is, we believe, the reality underlying all of these issues. You'll be expected to produce more in less time. You must constantly be learning new skills. You must acquire the facility of working comfortably with an incredibly diverse work force. Whatever job security you possess will come from your own resourcefulness and expertise. And you'll have to deal with international terrorism, urban violence, and global warming. The next century is not for the faint of heart!

Since you don't have any other century available to you, you'd best gear up. Here's what we know about resilience and coping with change.

Psychological Hardiness

In the 1970's, Salvatore Maddi and Suzanne Kobasa studied executives undergoing stress. More specifically, they studied a group of managers and executives in a large corporation which was undergoing reorganization. Reorganization means many jobs will change, and more than a few will be lost. In companies that reorganize, morale goes down and anxiety goes up. Will I have to change jobs? Will I have to let good people go? Will I be out on the street myself? If you keep up with the news at all, you know that corporate downsizing is virtually a way of life in the American workplace. (It turns out that the work of Maddi and Kobasa is extremely relevant to just about every person heading into the 21st Century.)

From *Learning for the 21st Century*, Fifth Edition by Bill Osher and Joann Ward. © 1996 by Bill Osher and Joann Ward.

During reorganization and downsizing, more people tend to get sick. They get more colds and cases of influenza. They get more migraines and back aches. And they have more ulcers and heart attacks. That's the bad news. The good news is that not everybody is equally vulnerable. Maddi and Kobasa found that some individuals were "psychologically hardy" (PH). These hardy individuals were sick less often and bounced back sooner after their illness. What makes them tick? The researchers identified several basic attitudes common to hardy individuals. You can think of them as the three C's:

1. An openness to *change,* viewing change as a challenge rather than a threat.

2. A high degree of *commitment* to what they do, demonstrating involvement in their activities and evidently relating them to life goals and objectives. Subjects low in commitment tended to be alienated from work, people, and social institutions.

3. A sense of *control* over most events encountered in life, rather than helplessness. High PH subjects were convinced they could influence the course of their lives. They believed their efforts made a difference at work, in school, and with other people. Low PH individuals were convinced they were powerless to influence outcomes. They tended to attribute what happened to their lives to forces outside themselves.

Individuals can respond to stressful events by coping actively or passively. High PH people see change as a challenge, make a commitment to get involved, and believe they have power to manage a difficult situation. Conversely, low PH people see change as a threat, avoid involvement, and feel powerless to cope. This leads them to deny the problems they face. They generally avoid their difficulties rather than confront them.

Change, obstacles, setbacks, and adversity are an inextricable part of living. The psychologically hardy person knows this, expects it, and thrives on actively engaging life. Every day brings new situations to handle, tasks to complete, events to manage. The high PH person meets life actively:

- Meets problems head on, doesn't escape, evade, or avoid.
- Believes struggle pays off. Working hard and smart pays.
- Believes (s)he has power to influence the outcome.
- Focuses on the situation.

The less psychologically hardy person meets life more passively:

- Runs from problems, escapes, evades, avoids, denies, blames.
- Is quick to give up. Doubts working harder or smarter pays.
- Doubts (s)he has the power to influence the outcome.
- Worries about the outcome.

In general, it is helpful to believe that you can manage the situation, solve the problem, climb the mountain. In one experiment, group A was asked to come up with as many solutions to a problem as they could. The one with the most viable solutions would be paid $10. Group B was asked to come up with X number of solutions (where X = average number of solutions of group A + 5). Group B reached significantly more viable solutions than Group A. Because the instructions implied they COULD reach more good solutions, they did. Some say defining a problem as a "problem" makes it harder to solve. Define it instead as a situation.

The Physiology of Stress

The diseases that do us in have changed over the course of history. Bubonic plague killed perhaps half of the population of Europe in the 14th Century. When Europeans came to the Americas in the 16th Century, they brought diseases to which the native Americans had no immunity. Large segments of the *indigenous* population died. As we approach the 21st Century, we have drastically reduced—especially in the developed world—the incidence of bubonic plague, cholera, small pox, diphtheria, and other infectious diseases. Yet humans today are still subject to premature death; it's just that the death will likely be stress-related instead of caused by bacterial or viral infection. Heart attacks, strokes, ulcers, and colitis: these are the diseases that will most likely kill us or slow us down today. While all of these conditions are the result of complex interactions between genetic predisposition, diet, and lifestyle, they differ from the diseases that laid our ancestors low in that germs are not their primary cause.

Humans have figured out reasonably well how to hold microbes in check, but they still haven't mastered modern stress with a body built for hunting/gathering and farming/herding. Imagine for a moment that you're a primitive cave dweller. You get up one fine day and lumber outside for some fresh air where you are confronted by a saber-toothed tiger. Immediately, your sympathetic nervous system triggers the fight-flight response. Adrenaline is pumped into your blood stream. Blood flows away from your extremities and into your larger muscles. (If the tiger claws your hand or forearm, you will less likely bleed to death.) Your pupils dilate, enabling you quickly to see large, uncomplicated threats (such as charging tigers). Your breathing is rapid and shallow. You are prepared to run from physical danger or confront it with your club. You're in a dangerous situation, but your body is doing everything it can to help you survive.

Now, imagine you're a premed student. You walk into your organic chemistry final feeling not too confident. If you bomb this exam, you'll make a C in the class. If you ace it, you'll make an A. The A means med school. The C means selling medical supplies. Your body again springs into action. Blood leaves your extremities. (That's why your hands are cold.) Your pupils dilate, your breathing grows shallow and rapid, and your mind races. The trouble is that your body is preparing you better to face simple, physical threats than the complex, abstract ones which in fact populate your universe. You might feel like poking your professor in the nose or running out of the classroom screaming, but fighting or running are much more effective against tigers than against professors.

Unless you learn to respond appropriately to the complexities of modern life, you will not perform as well as you'd like. But that's only a part of the problem. Each time your body prepares you to run from danger or fight it, it's a strain on your body. After the danger passes, the parasympathetic nervous system kicks in and restores your body's equilibrium. But let's suppose that after equilibrium is restored, you're faced with another threat, precipitating another fight-flight response. And about the time that one dies out, another threat comes along, then another. At some point, your parasympathetic nervous system stops restoring your body's equilibrium. You're in a near constant state of vigilance: pumped up, wired, and ready for physical danger. You're also on course for an early heart attack.

All this is to say that it's in your interest to learn to manage stress like a citizen of the 21st Century rather than Og, Son of Fire. If you do, you will perform more effectively in today's rapidly changing, complexity-filled world. You will also do so for a longer period of time. Consider carefully the following tips for managing stress.

Stress Management Checklist

1. **Manage your time and organize your things**—two sure ways to reduce your headaches and save your stomach lining.

2. **Don't spread yourself too thin.** See number 3.

3. **Learn to say "no."** See number 2.

4. **Cultivate friends as well as contacts.**

5. **Participate in at least one extracurricular activity** because you enjoy it, not because it's going to pay off down the road.

6. **Do something fun every day.**

7. **Exercise regularly.** The busier you are, the more important this one is.

8. **Eat sensibly.**

9. **Get enough sleep.**

10. **Learn to relax.** We've included instructions at the end of this chapter for Deep Muscle Relaxation and Guided Imagery, but biofeedback, yoga, and meditation are also effective tension reducers for most people.

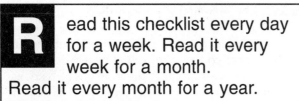

R ead this checklist every day for a week. Read it every week for a month. Read it every month for a year. Repeat as needed.

Recently we heard a psychologist refer to the very competitive university where he worked as a Type-A factory. Type-A individuals are goal directed, driven people who get a lot done, but find it difficult to relax. They are also heart attack prone.

Recent research by health psychologist Margaret Chesney, however, suggested that it is possible to be achievement oriented without the heart attack. The key is in your attitude. Anger and hostility seem to be much more injurious to your heart than ambition and hard work. The most deadly combination of all is the Type A who is unassertive and very angry. This person is too passive to get his/her own way very often, so (s)he spends a lot of time feeling frustrated and mad. And because (s)he lacks the ability to express himself assertively, (s)he has no constructive way of communicating pent-up feelings.

It would appear, then, that you can strive toward your goals if you're flexible about doing so. Frequent frustration and anger are the tip-offs that you're not keeping things in perspective. *If college life seems too hectic, see a counselor.*

In conclusion, we offer two final bits of advice. Repeat them whenever the stress starts to mount:

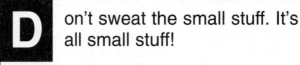

D on't sweat the small stuff. It's all small stuff!

Deep Muscle Relaxation Instructions

Find a quiet place and get into a comfortable position. Your bed or an easy chair is usually conducive to relaxing. Take your time when you practice DMR. Hurrying defeats the purpose. After you get more skilled at relaxing, you can learn to speed the technique up. Most people get better results if they close their eyes while practicing this technique.

The entire exercise should take ten or more minutes, but with practice you can learn to relax in seconds.

Guided Imagery Instructions

Find a quiet, comfortable place and close your eyes. Imagine that you're resting securely on a beautiful, deserted beach. Beyond the white sand is azure water with gentle, rolling waves. Feel the warmth of the sun on your skin, the caress of the breeze in your hair, the grainy texture of the sand between your toes. Relax. Listen to the sound of the surf. Watch the rhythm of the waves as they rise and fall. Take in a deep breath of fresh air and relax deeply as you exhale. Notice a flock of gulls hovering above the waves. Study the slow, graceful movement of the wings of one of the birds. Watch the bird's wings gradually slow down. Yet it stays airborne, seemingly without effort. Become as relaxed as the bird.

Again the entire fantasy should take ten or more minutes. Following DMR with a relaxing mental scene often deepens the sense of calm, so experiment with combining the two methods. Practice is, of course, essential. Remember, relaxation isn't a luxury. It's a necessity. Money and position mean very little if you're not healthy.

Using Relaxation Techniques Situationally

Relax by using DMR or imagery. Once you're calm and tension free, you can prepare for any stressful task, such as a test or important interview. Simply imagine yourself handling the test effectively. Should you start to feel any tension or anxiety, redirect your attention to the beach scene (or whatever scene is most relaxing to you) until you regain your composure. Keep repeating until you can easily imagine yourself handling the task in question.

On the day of the test, be sure to show up at class on time. While the test is being passed out, quietly relax using the techniques you've mastered. Should you get flustered or find your mind racing during the test, simply pause and take a couple of minutes to relax.

1. Make tight fists out of both your hands. Study the tension in your hands. Now, let it go. Allow every muscle fiber in your hands to grow limp and calm. Notice that we say "allow." You can't really relax by trying harder.

2. Repeat this pattern with each muscle group in your body. Next, do your forearms.

3. Upper arms.

4. Shoulders and neck.

5. Forehead.

6. Eyes.

7. Lips.

8. Jaw.

9. Chest.

10. Abdomen.

11. Upper legs.

12. Lower legs.

13. Feet.

Organizing Your Time and Setting Priorities

Due to the many demands that we are expected to fulfill on a daily basis, the need to efficiently manage your time is extremely important. Good organizational skills are necessary to any plan of time management. One of the recommended strategies is to establish priorities on a "to do" checklist. The higher the value you assign to an event, the higher its priority on the checklist. This checklist allows you to preview the day before it begins, giving you control over which events will be addressed in which sequence during that day. It may be necessary, on occasion, to shift your focus from meeting the demands of an important event, to addressing issues of importance that might arise spontaneously. You need to be flexible to avoid stress when you cannot control every event that may occur and when it may occur. Other recommendations for time management might include the use of the types of daily planners, appointment books and/or software packages suggested in Chapter Two.

Building a System of Support

All support can be divided into both internal and external resources. Internal resources are those that lie within us (morals, personal philosophies, spirituality, etc.) and are the basis for us addressing our own challenges without outside intervention (help from a friend, guidance as a parent, campus resources, etc.). It is important that the people you choose as resources share your values. For example, talk to a friend who is supportive of your college goals when you are struggling with the demands of classes. Your decision to be supported in your time of need is a direct reflection of your desire to take control of your life.

> **T**ake advantage of all of the resources available to you to support your quest for academic and personal success.

The following on-campus resources are designed to support your desire for student success:

The **Office of Student Support Services** serves as the information and referral service to answer any questions students have regarding policies and procedures. Student Advisors are available to help students with any problems that may affect their ability to be successful in school. The Advisors also assist with curriculum planning and monitoring degree progress.

The **Academic Skills Center** (ASC) provides a wide range of personalized services such as individual tutoring, computer and Internet access, developmental and enrichment courses and study skills workshops. The ASC also has peer tutors available who are trained to assist fellow students in their technology.

The **Office of Career Services** offers a number of services related to employment and careers. Those services include assistance with resume writing, interview skills and searching for a job while in school or for a career after graduation.

The **Financial Aid Office** oversees federal and state student financial aid programs and assists students in applying for financial aid. Financial aid at New England Tech is available through various sources: grants and scholarship programs, work-study programs, student loans, institutional payment plans and private loans.

The **Office of Teaching and Learning** oversees all educational aspects of the college. It is responsible for faculty, curricula, academic policies and graduation requirements.

■ Staying Motivated

Motivation is an internal desire satisfied by something we think, feel or do. Your success in meeting your goals will be strongly influenced by the passion and excitement you experience on behalf of your goal. The greater the benefit that you derive from accomplishing your goal, the more motivated you will become. Thus, motivation becomes the conduit between goal setting and goal accomplishment. When you assign a high degree of relevancy to a goal, the potential for excitement and passion increases measurably, thereby making the goal more accomplishable. The next reading provides additional information about the topic of motivation.

■ Reading: What Makes Achievers Tick?

Successful people are achievers, but what makes them go? Great tomes have been written on the psychology of achievement. We believe all this material can be boiled down to one short sentence: achievers are goal directed. Goal and Direction. Let's take a look at each.

Goals

1. **Achievers set goals.** They aim for excellence: building a better "widget," writing an A term paper, instilling a love of learning in first-graders.

2. **Achievers set *clear* goals.** There is a difference between dreams and plans. Anyone can fantasize about fame and fortune, but a plan requires concrete, specific objectives to shoot for. The most effective people take the trouble to make their goals clear. Too many students say, "I'm going to get a lot of studying done this weekend," or "I want to make it big in the business world." The true achievers more likely say, "I'm going to study history for two hours Saturday morning and work math problems for two hours on Sunday afternoon," or "I'm going to major in electrical engineering so I can eventually develop computer hardware." When you set clear goals, you can tell whether you're really making progress. If you are, success is a powerful motivator. If not, you can adjust your plans.

> **A**nyone can fantasize about fame and fortune, but a plan requires concrete, specific objectives to shoot for.

3. **Achievers set *realistic* goals.** Their goals demand talent and effort, but they are doable. The most successful people don't generally take long shots. They don't depend on luck. Achievers like a challenge with some risk, but not the probability of failure.

One way psychologists have studied achievement is to watch subjects compete at a ringtoss game. If points are awarded based on distance from the target, players who throw from medium range almost always win the most points. They also reveal the highest drive for success on other measures. And, most importantly they tend to be the best students, the most effective salespeople, the most successful entrepreneurs.

From *Learning for the 21st Century*, Fifth Edition by Bill Osher and Joann Ward. © 1996 by Bill Osher and Joann Ward.

Underachievers go after ridiculously easy goals or impossibly difficult ones. Achievers like a challenge, but they don't want to be overwhelmed. They aim for goals of moderate difficulty. Then, as soon as they reach them, they set their sights one notch higher.

4. **Achievers set long-term, intermediate, and short-term goals.** Successful entrepreneurs often have five-year plans, quarterly goals, and a weekly calendar. The best students operate similarly.

Direction

Direction implies action, movement, getting things done, making things happen. The director of a movie, more than anyone else, determines the quality of the film. A director is in charge.

Achievers are also in charge. They don't wait passively for success to come their way. They strive to reach their goals. Here's how:

1. **Achievers think a lot about their goals and how to reach them.** They daydream about them, juggling strategies and weighing alternatives. Since they think about how to reach their goals so much of the time, they come up with a lot of shortcuts, improvements, and better methods.

   Just about everyone dreams of success. The true achievers go one step farther—they dream how to make it happen!

2. **Achievers plan.** They're more time conscious. They set objectives and deadlines on paper and keep score of how they're doing. This is why we urge you to use daily to-do lists and to map out your assignments for an entire semester.

3. **Achievers prioritize.** Working hard and getting lots of things done may not be enough if you neglect something important. It's getting the most important things done that makes you truly successful.

4. **Achievers take it step by step.** They implement the good plans they make. They break up large tasks into smaller ones. A year-long project can be divided into a series of shorter deadlines. A college education can be divided into four years, each year into semesters, each semester into weeks. A term paper can be similarly chopped up into manageable tasks.

5. **Achievers overcome barriers.** When they run into roadblocks, they keep trying till they find a way to get around them. Naturally, they can get discouraged too, but they bounce back from defeat rather than letting it keep them down. If personal shortcomings hold them back, they find a way to compensate or they change. They never wait to be rescued. They actively seek out expert help whenever it's needed to get the job done.

One of our greatest satisfactions is watching college students develop. We've seen country bumpkins overcome their lack of sophistication. We've seen shy students join clubs so they can learn to conduct a meeting. We've known premeds who managed to eke out Bs in calculus because they studied overtime and hired a tutor.

Successful people come in all shapes and sizes. One thing they have in common is that they don't easily take "no" for an answer. They're not quick to throw in the towel. They encounter their share of setbacks, but they keep on keeping on.

We recall one young woman from a rural background whose father had died when she was a child. Her mother discouraged her from applying to a competitive college. She filled out the forms by herself and also applied for financial aid. When she arrived on campus, she felt out of place, and she had to struggle to survive in class. Her boyfriend kept after her to transfer to the junior college in her hometown. Besides, who needed a college degree? She could always clerk in the local dime store. With some difficulty, she broke things off with her old boyfriend. She joined a study group, and that helped her with her grades. She got counseling to improve her self-confidence. She had to work part-time to make ends meet. At first, she waited tables, but eventually she did drafting for a small engineering company. She finally managed to graduate and began working full-time for the same firm.

It wasn't a very good job. Her attempts at finding a better one didn't lead to much, so she got help from her college's career planning center. She developed a better job search plan and improved her resume. She was discouraged to discover she was no longer eligible to set up interviews through the campus placement center. But she didn't give up. She began dropping by the placement office at noon and started having lunch with the corporate recruiters. Within a few months she had been invited to interview with several companies. She received several offers and accepted the one she felt was best for her.

We are proud to know this woman who was born into near poverty. Her family and friends advised her against pursuing her dreams. She made mistakes, and she encountered innumerable barriers to success. But she didn't give up.

Today, she is an engineer for a Fortune 500 corporation. She designs radar systems for supersonic aircraft.

It's All Up to You

There is a ten-word phrase which contains the secret of your success. Just to make it more challenging, each of the ten words is a two-letter word. The fifth and tenth words rhyme. Can you create the phrase? The phrase appears at the end of this chapter.

If you want success you've got to believe it's up to you to go out and get it.

Who determines your destiny? You? Or is your future controlled by forces outside yourself? Your answers to these questions have a powerful influence on what you accomplish. If you believe you control your future, psychologists say you have an internal "locus of control." If you believe you're a passive victim to what fate brings, they say you possess an external "locus of control."

We believe the foundation of all achievement lies in believing that planning and effort can influence the future. So, are you the kind of person who lays plans to open a business in five years? Or do you figure, "Why bother? Something will go wrong. It always does." Can you pass up the Monday Night Movie in order to fine tune your resume? Or do you think, "It's not worth it. You've got to have connections to work for that company." Do you study harder after a bad grade? Or do you say, "It doesn't do any good to prepare for that teacher's tests, anyway."

How to Get More Go

Chances are, you believe you can strongly influence your own future. You probably are the kind of person who is motivated to achieve or you wouldn't have read this far. But suppose you're not. You might be reading this chapter because it's required for a course. And now you're convinced that you're very externally oriented and have very little in common with achievers. Well, don't despair. You can change.

Research psychologist George Burris taught underachieving college students some of the same principles we've outlined in this chapter. In just one semester he got results. Achievement motivation scores went up, and so did grades. Another psychologist, Richard DeCharms, worked with teachers of disadvantaged children. He emphasized that they work to develop an internal locus of control in their students. And the students' grades improved significantly.

DeCharms has developed an innovative way of thinking about power and achievement. He says people tend to be either Pawns or Origins. Pawns are passive, generally acted upon, and don't have much control over their future. Origins, on the other hand, actively determine what happens to them.

You can take the Pawn analogy one step further—individuals can be compared to the pieces in the game of chess. A pawn is the least powerful piece. Basically, a pawn can move straight ahead, one square at a time. It enjoys very little choice or power. When confronted with an obstacle, it can only wait until the obstacle is removed.

If, however, a pawn is passed all the way to the end of the board, it can be exchanged for a queen. A queen can move vertically, horizontally, or diagonally. It can go forward or backward for as many squares as there are on the board. Talk about controlling your own destiny! The queen has the whole board to play with. The pawn has just one square.

Suppose a queen mistakenly thought she was a pawn. Her choices would be drastically limited. Conversely, if a pawn started acting like a queen, the sky would be the limit.

Why do some people become pawns and others become queens? Why do some students feel powerless to influence their futures, while others are convinced their efforts can make a difference?

Any kind of oppression undermines the development of motivation. Oppression can be blatant, like racism or poverty. It can be as subtle as overprotective parents. But it's too late to change where you grew up or how your parents raised you.

So what can you do if you want to achieve more? First, as simple as it sounds, you've got to believe that your own efforts make a difference.

If we haven't convinced you, please talk to a counselor. Virtually all counselors are committed to helping their clients become more independent, more in charge of their own lives.

Second, follow the suggestions in this book. We didn't pull them out of a hat. Our ideas come directly from the experts on achievement motivation, such as Harvard's David McClelland. Look at the Table of Contents. Every chapter has to do with planning, organizing, developing skills, using resources, and setting goals.

We can't make you follow our suggestions, but we urge you to try them. They work. Your performance will improve. You'll taste success. And success breeds success. We guarantee it. Here's a way to assess your own motive to achieve.

> **S**o what can you do if you want to achieve more? First, as simple as it sounds, you've got to believe that your own efforts make a difference.

> **T**he secret of your success: If it is to be, it is up to me.

■ Quick-Scoring Achievement Motivation Quiz

Points   **Score**

1. <u>0</u>   I have no clear goals in life.
   <u>1</u>   I have a general idea of a career in which I want to succeed.
   <u>2</u>   I set daily objectives which advance me toward my long-term goals.
   <u>3</u>   I set daily, weekly, and quarterly goals which will advance me toward my
           long-term goals.   _____

2. <u>0</u>   I'm too proud to accept help, no matter how stuck or lost I get.
   <u>1</u>   I will accept help, but only when it's offered.
   <u>2</u>   I actively seek out expert help whenever I get stuck or lost.
   <u>3</u>   I am acquainted with most campus resources and regularly use them
           without becoming dependent upon them.   _____

3. <u>0</u>   I tend to give up after the first setback.
   <u>1</u>   I eventually bounce back from a setback after a period of immobilization.
   <u>2</u>   I analyze my setbacks instead of kicking myself or blaming others.
   <u>3</u>   A setback inspires me to try again, using new methods if needed.   _____

4. <u>0</u>   My fantasies about career success are limited to scenes from "Lifestyles of
           the Rich and Famous."
   <u>1</u>   My fantasies about career success include practical details of my future
           world of work.
   <u>2</u>   My fantasies about career success include thinking about steps I can take
           on a daily basis.
   <u>3</u>   My fantasies about career success include long-range, intermediate, and
           daily plans to reach my goals.   _____

5. <u>0</u>   Most of my goals are so high that I seldom reach them or so low that
           I reach them with very little effort.
   <u>1</u>   At least some of my goals are moderately difficult—high enough to
           challenge me but low enough not to overwhelm me with anxiety.
   <u>2</u>   Most of my goals are moderately difficult.
   <u>3</u>   Most of my goals are moderately difficult, and I increase their difficulty as
           I reach them.   _____

   TOTAL   _____

Scoring:

0 Points   If you don't crawl out from under the doormat and start moving, you will be overwhelmed in the 21st Century.

1–5 Points   You're taking the first steps toward success. Still a way to go, though.

6–10 Points You're on the way, but watch out—success can be addictive.

11–15 Points The stuff of champions. You're on your way to succeeding in the 21st Century.

■ Summary

- In order to take control of your life, you must cope with change.
- Relaxation and maintaining perspective are necessary skills in self-management.
- It is important to organize your time and set priorities.
- You need to build a system of support both on-campus and off-campus.
- Your short- and long-term goals require that you stay motivated or understand how to become motivated.

Additional Resources

Resources in the Learning Resources Center (call numbers are shown in parentheses after the citation):

Carter, C. & Kravits, S. L. (1996). *Keys to success: how to achieve your goals.* Upper Saddle River, NJ: Prentice Hall. (LB2343.32 .C37 1996)

Corey, G. (1990). *I never knew I had a choice.* Pacific Grove, CA: Brooks/Cole Pub. Co. (BF697.5 .S43 C67 1990)

Hansen, R. S. & Hansen, K. (1997). *Write your way to a higher GPA: how to dramatically boost your GPA simply by sharpening your writing skills.* Berkeley, CA: Ten Speed Press. (PE1408 .H329 1997)

Jasper, J. (1999). *Take back your time: how to regain control of work, information, and technology.* New York: St. Martin's Griffin. (HD69 .T54 J37 1999)

O'Keefe, E. J. (1993). *Self-management for college students: the ABC approach.* Hyde Park, NY: Partridge Hill Publishers. (LB1065 .O36 1993)

Roberts, J. M. (1999). *Effective study skills: maximizing your academic potential.* Upper Saddle River, NJ: Prentice Hall. (LB2395 .R63 1999)

Silber, L. T. (1998). *Time management for the creative person.* New York: Three Rivers Press. (HD69 .T54 S575 1998)

Web Sites:

Please note that Web site addresses often change. If you are unable to reach the addresses below, use a search engine and search the source of the site or the title of the Web document to find the new site.

Motivation
University of Texas at Austin, Learning Skills Center:
    http://www.utexas.edu/student/lsc/handouts/1903.html
University of Victoria, Learning Skills Program:
    http://www.coun.uvic.ca/learn/motivate.html
Mental Help Net: http://mentalhelp.net/psyhelp/chap4/

On-Campus Resources:

Academic Skills Center, Center for the Technologies, Third Floor, (401) 739-5000, Ext. 3416.

Financial Aid Office, Gouse Building, First Floor, (401) 739-5000, Ext. 3354.

Office of Career Services, Center for the Technologies, Second Floor, (401) 739-5000, Ext. 3458.

Office of Student Support Services, Baywood Building, (401) 739-5000, Ext. 3441.

Office of Teaching and Learning, Greenwood Building, First Floor, (401) 739- 5000, Ext. 3333.

Activities

4-1 Reflect on the concepts presented in class, in the case study at the end of this chapter and in the discussion and think of how you can apply these coping strategies in your own life.

4-2 Apply the information from the learning objectives of this chapter to the goals you have identified (to both short-term and long-term goals). Answering the following questions will help you to complete your self-assessment required at the end of this course:

1. How will you adapt to any stressors or cope with change as you move toward your goals?

2. What will you do to relax and keep a healthy perspective during this time?

3. How will you organize your time and establish priorities?

4. What is your support system? How will you establish or strengthen it?

5. Describe what you do to stay motivated.

■ Activity 4-1. Case Study

Read the Following Case Study

"Either you've got it or you don't—street smarts I've got, academic smarts I don't," Ernie would say. Growing up, Ernie thought studious types were bores. He never imagined himself a student, but when the opportunity to go to college presented itself, Ernie thought he'd give it a shot. "A college degree is a sure ticket to a good job," he explained to one of his buddies, who was puzzled by Ernie's decision to go to school.

Life doesn't come easy for Ernie—it is a stressful series of demands. Just before exams, he plows through his readings a second time, marking the few remaining spaces that haven't seen his yellow highlighter. When a paper is due, he stays up all night if he has to. A push on the computer spell check button is Ernie's idea of revision. To complicate matters, Ernie has a low-paying job at a minimum wage, is the single parent of a two-year-old, is living with his parents and is determined to complete school as his ticket to both personal and financial independence. One day, a professor asked him, "Why are you in college?" Surprised by the question, Ernie wasn't sure what to say. "Same as anyone else—to get a job," he mumbled. "Do yourself a favor and forget the job; educate yourself first," the professor responded, "and you'll be better prepared to meet the demands of your life."

Each of the following questions relates to the topics discussed in today's class regarding taking control of your life. In small groups, discuss and respond to each item. Your group should record the responses and be prepared to discuss them with the class. (Tip: You might choose to identify or list Ernie's demands before responding to the question.)

Coping:
How can Ernie cope with the many circumstances that he is dealing with, without abandoning any of the demands?

Relaxation:
What techniques can Ernie use so that he can maintain a "cool head" in the face of what he's dealing with?

Organization:
How can Ernie "juggle" all of his demands so that none are left unaddressed?

Support:
Where would Ernie turn to for the help he would need in managing his demands?

Motivation:
In the face of Ernie's challenges, how can he maintain interest in his school work?

CHAPTER 5
Assessing Your Computer Competency

"We both came to New England Tech because a friend of ours had gone here and now has a great job. The instructors are wonderful, and we really enjoyed the classes. The college has had a tremendous impact on both our lives. We now have great jobs at Intel in Hudson, MA!"

Joseph Sousa and Jeffrey Desrosiers
Electronics Technology

Chapter Designers:

Doreen Lasiewski, Director of Instructional Development
Louise Hamelin, Coordinator of Computer Services, Academic Skills Center

What Students Are Saying . . .

"The evaluation on computer competency was very useful for me. I was able to identify several areas of computer competency I needed help with. As a result I have enrolled in a computer class for next quarter that covers keyboarding to Internet use."

David Rymeski
Computer Networking and Servicing Technology

In This Chapter

You will become familiar with and be able to describe the interface between learning and technology.

You will identify the computer skills needed in your Quarter One classes.

■ Introduction

Regardless of your career plans, computers are sure to be important tools and resources in obtaining your goals. This chapter will provide you with an opportunity to assess your level of computer skill competency. In the process, you will identify the computer skills needed to successfully complete Quarter One of your technology and strategies to improve your computer skills.

The Academic Skills Center (ASC) at New England Institute of Technology provides support services in an environment designed to increase your comfort level and improve your level of computer skill competency. These services include computers available for student use, computer skill specialists to tutor you with specific computer software needs, an ASC web-site with helpful tips and tools and course work to provide instruction in hardware, software and computer applications.

■ The Interface Between Learning and Computer Technology

Being computer literate is essential in meeting the demands of the new millennium. Having knowledge and understanding of computers and their uses becomes a valuable tool to use in many areas of our daily lives, especially in the areas of business and education. To be successful, today's students must have some level of computer literacy.

How Do Technology and Education Go Together?

Since the mid-1980s, the connection between technology and education has become increasingly important. It is almost impossible to obtain a good education without using some form of computer technology. There are very few schools at any level that can get by without exposing their students to a wide variety of educational software packages.

Computer software is used to educate, to entertain and to communicate with the rest of the world.

It is quite common for elementary and secondary schools to use computer-assisted software packages to assist students who need individualized help. Software also exists that teaches specific concepts and that serve as a drill for young students. Many parents purchase software for their children that is both entertaining and educational. Now, it is not at all unusual for youngsters to teach their parents to use computers.

Computers, and more specifically the Internet, are beginning to shrink the world and make it nearly as easy for American children to communicate with children in China as it is to communicate with a friend who lives down the street. The Internet is a vehicle for students to learn a variety of skills necessary in the workplace of the future. With the Internet, diversity and technology are becoming an accepted part of our daily lives.

In addition to the important links between education and technology mentioned above, computers have now become indispensable to the world of research. There are few libraries in any educational institution that can get by without having some sort of electronic reference tools, an online catalog or Internet access. The ability to tap into databases worldwide at relatively low cost has revolutionized teaching in schools and libraries.

How Does Technology Fit Into the Workplace?

Technology has also revolutionized the way that we communicate with each other and exchange information. The workplace of the 21st Century demands a high degree of written, spoken and technological skill in order to compete successfully. There are very few jobs today that do not require at least some use of computers. Business, retail and service occupations rely heavily upon computers to communicate, to maintain and store data, to analyze the performance of humans or computer-controlled machines and to conduct research.

There are many ways to exchange information in the workplace that require well-developed skills:

- E-mail: Information becomes available to another if thoughts can be expressed clearly, concisely and in a grammatically correct manner. Writing skills will be strengthened by the course work within your academic courses. The computer skills needed in utilizing software and hardware to send messages (possibly with attachments) will be learned throughout your academic experience.
- Fax: Similarly, letters, documents and memos sent by fax machines provide information in a written format. The skills necessary to compose clear documents will be learned in academic and technical classrooms.
- Phone: Expressing yourself verbally in a professional or proper social manner are skills to be learned. Classroom discussions and formal presentations provide an opportunity to gain the confidence and experience you need to succeed.
- Printed documents: As with other forms of communication, printed documents need to be written clearly and correctly. The availability of sophisticated word processing software as well as the relatively low cost of high-quality printers makes it increasingly important to have the skills to produce not only readable but aesthetically pleasing documents.

What Are Some Important Computer Skills to Learn?

- ■ Operational skills: Being knowledgeable in the utilization of an operating system and the hardware devices is critical to technical success. These skills would include how to start a computer, open a software package, create and save files and print a document.
- ■ Keyboarding Skills: Being familiar with the location of letters, numbers and function keys reduces the time it takes to complete a computer task.
- ■ Internet Skills: Essential for retrieving information quickly.
- ■ Software Packages: Mastering word processing, spreadsheet and/or database software will enhance your employability and help you to manage your life.

Computer skills are not only needed throughout the course of your education and in your career; but often bridge the gap between the unemployed and the employed. Many employers conduct searches for qualified individuals through the Internet. Because of the low cost of posting a job on the Internet compared to publishing it in a newspaper, many job ads now appear exclusively on the Internet. What does this mean to you? Well, it means that if you have well-developed computer skills you may be able to search for and apply for a job using a computer, gaining advantage over others that do not have those computer skills.

■ Reading: The Seven Principles of the Information Age

1. Knowledge is power. In the Information Age, strength and power are related to knowledge. The strongest countries are those with the best educational systems, which produce the best scientists, technicians, and managers. Japan, for example, is a small, crowded island nation with relatively few natural resources. Yet, its economy is very strong because its educational system produces technically skilled citizens, with very few falling through the cracks. When compared with Japan, the United States' high school dropout and illiteracy rates make it very difficult for us to compete industrially as a nation. The strongest corporations are those which attract and cultivate intellectual talent and know how to nurture its expression. Currently, it is considered vital for any business enterprise to be "a learning organization."

In the Information Age, the height of your career ladder will be largely determined by the depth and breadth of your knowledge. College is probably the best chance you'll ever have to strengthen and lengthen that ladder.

The implications of this truth are profound. If you want to prosper in the next century, you must do it with your brain. That means attending college and getting one or more degrees is more important than it has ever been. The 1992 U.S. Census reports the following correlation between education and income:

From *Learning for the 21st Century,* Fifth Edition by Bill Osher and Joann Ward. © 1998 by Bill Osher and Joann Ward. Reprinted with permission of Kendall/Hunt Publishing Company.

Household Income

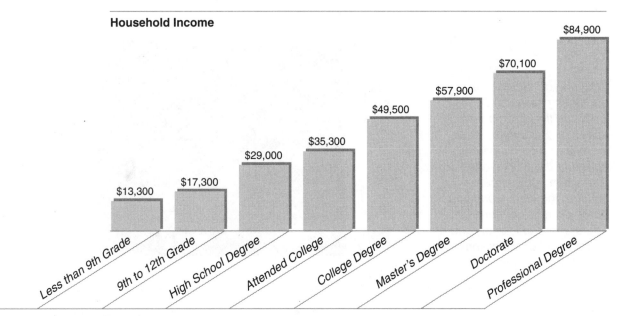

Educational Attainment

Education has been related to success for many years. Its significance today is even more profound. Russell Jacoby observes in *Dogmatic Wisdom, How the Culture Wars Divert Education and Distract America* that in the 1970s white college graduates earned only 18 percent more than white male high school graduates. By 1989, the difference had shot up to 45 percent. For women and blacks the difference is even more striking. By 1989 the white women college graduates earned 75 percent more than their high school graduate counterparts. In that same year, African-American female college graduates made 92 percent more than their high school graduate peers.

Of course, education is about much more than getting a string of degrees. What really counts is learning how to learn and becoming a continuous learner throughout your life. Ed Cornish, in the January/February 1996 edition of *The Futurist*, predicts that education may become compulsory for adults as well as young people.

2. The pace of life will accelerate. If anything characterizes contemporary society, it is speed. Time is already money in today's world. Meeting deadlines, working overtime, doing business in a "New York minute"—these are common practices today. Federal Express was built on the need of businesses to deliver fast. This trend will only increase in the 21st Century. Letters used to take months. Now they take only a few days, but that's still not fast enough. That's why people now use e-mail instead of "snail mail." The phone and the FAX carry information at the speed of light. One way to represent the speed that characterizes contemporary life is through the speed with which computer chips process information. The October 1995 *National Geographic* devoted an entire article to the Information Revolution. That in itself is revealing: cyberspace has in a sense become the geography of our time. Among the observations made was the breathtakingly rapid increasing speed of computers: In 1971, a chip could perform 60,000 "additions" per second; in 1974, 290,000; in 1979, 330,000; in 1982, 900,000; in 1985, 5.5 million; in 1989, 20 million; in 1993, 100 million; in 1995, 250 million "additions" per second. In 25 years, the speed of computers has increased four thousand fold!

As smaller chips are manufactured with more circuits, computers get faster and smaller. As computers become faster and smaller, they become more portable and more affordable. As portability and affordability increase, so does the speed with which business and industry is conducted. We are traveling into the 21st Century with the foot of society firmly pressing the accelerator to the floorboard.

Why do you care about additions per second? Because the volume and speed of the computer has increased the volume and speed of the work world. And when you get out of college, the work world you enter will require more hours, more efficiency, and a higher level of educational sophistication than people in previous decades. And, as the volume and speed of computers increase so does our capability as a society. The flip side of that coin is, how does it eventually affect our humanity?

The computer chips of 1971 calculated in "additions" per second, at a rate approximately proportional to the period at the end of this sentence.

A decade later, the computer chips of 1982 calculated in "additions" per second are approximately proportional to the block below.

Not quite 25 years since that "period" at the end of the sentence above, our present computer chips calculate "additions" per second at a rate approximately proportional to the screen of this computer.

3. Change will be pervasive. Technological innovation will constantly alter our lives. In the early days of the television industry, three networks broadcast programs to a few thousand viewers in one country. With cable television, there were dozens of channels pumping out information to millions of customers across the world. Soon there will be hundreds of channels. Nations, industries, and companies rise and fall. Those who best cope with constant change will endure and prosper. Joel Baker in *Future Edge* recounts the following true story of the challenges and opportunities associated with change. In 1968, Switzerland dominated the watchmaking industry worldwide. They made the best watches. They worked unceasingly to improve them. It was understandable then that they would garner 80 percent to 90 percent of the industry's profits worldwide. Yet, by 1980, the Swiss' profit share had dropped to less than 20 percent. Why? Because they did not adjust rapidly enough to change.

What happened? The Japanese adopted and developed the electronic quartz movement, and that became the benchmark of the watchmaking industry. What makes this story so ironic is that it was the Swiss themselves who invented the technology. Their corporate leaders, however, did not anticipate the changing demands of their customers and so rejected this technological innovation. Japan now leads the world in the sale of timepieces.

4. We will be overwhelmed with information. In *Little Science, Big Science,* Derek Price charts the phenomenal accelerating growth of scientific knowledge in the last few hundred years. In the middle of the 17th Century there were two scientific journals. One hundred years later there were ten. Fifty years after that there were one hundred. Fifty years after that, 1,000. By 1963, there were approximately 50,000! Presumably, there are over 100,000 scientific journals regularly published as we approach the 21st Century. This means that scientific knowledge doubles every few years. Petersen, in *The Road to 2015,* guestimates it doubles every 18 months. It's extremely difficult to keep up with all the advances in any one field. It's impossible to keep up with the advances in all fields. There's even a term for this state of affairs. It's called information overload.

Petersen further observes that a person who reads an entire copy of the Sunday *New York Times* would take in more information in one afternoon than the average citizen in Thomas Jefferson's day would within a lifetime. There are many implications to the problem posed by information overload. Which information do we regard as essential to pass on to the next generation? What core knowledge must college students master? How can you as a citizen stay informed? How can you as a professional keep abreast of your field?

5. Diversity will dominate. We live in a global economy, buying, selling, and trading with every part of the world. The planet will continue to shrink as transportation grows faster and instantaneous communication networks reach all areas of the globe. It is highly likely that you will work outside of the continental United States at some point during your career. You will be called upon to do business with people whose culture, language, and beliefs differ from yours. The composition of the American workforce is also growing more diverse. By the year 2000, the percentage of white non-Hispanic men, historically the largest segment comprising our labor force, will shrink, while the percentage of African-American, Asian, and Hispanic job holders will rise. Women of all races will account for almost half of the labor force in the U.S. Your colleagues will be of African, Hispanic, European, and Asian origins, as well as mixtures thereof. Historically, career women could choose between nursing and teaching. Today, women are entering science and engineering, law and medicine, management and the executive suite. You will work for and with women.

Ired Forum, a publication of the Geneva-based Development Innovations and Networks, captures the flavor of the future by creating an imaginary village of 1,000 people to represent the **demographics** of the entire planet. In this village, there would be:

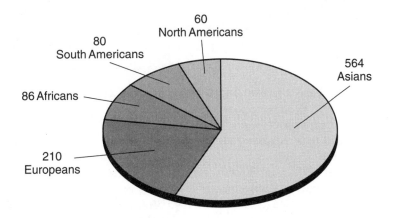

There would be:

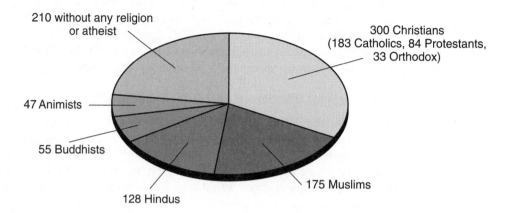

210 without any religion or atheist

300 Christians (183 Catholics, 84 Protestants, 33 Orthodox)

47 Animists

55 Buddhists

128 Hindus

175 Muslims

While the planet as a whole has always been characterized by racial, cultural, and ethnic diversity, this variety has a much greater impact upon us today because telecommunications and transportation have eroded most of the national and geographical barriers that historically have separated us. I (Bill) live in Atlanta, Georgia, a scant few years ago the heart of the deep South. When I finish this chapter I will drive to the Dekalb International Farmers Market, which serves a thoroughly international customer base and is staffed by employees from every continent. Each employee wears a name tag indicating the various languages that he or she speaks. I can buy collard greens, pork chops, and catfish. I can also buy squid, jicama, and lemon grass. This Farmers Market is a snapshot of the future demographics of the United States.

6. The secure, lifetime job will be a thing of the past. Employees won't work for a giant corporation over a thirty year career that culminates in a retirement dinner and a gold watch. People will have many jobs and a number of careers. Some would say that the traditional job is an endangered species. Downsizing has become a way of life in the corporate world, affecting blue-collar and white collar employees alike. More and more people will manage their own careers, selling their expertise to a variety of individuals and organizations as self-employed entrepreneurs.

7. Enormous challenges loom ahead. As the world population grows on a planet that doesn't, there are numerous obstacles to peace and prosperity looming on the horizon: overpopulation, environmental degradation, violence, disease, and poverty. Any one of these issues could fill a book if not an entire library, but that is beyond the scope of this text.

So there it is. You are closing in on the 21st Century. You will face a strikingly different world than your parents faced. Can you keep up with rapidly changing technology? Will you flounder in an ocean of information? What will the world of work be like? How will you manage your career? Will public schools be good enough to educate your children? Will your confidence in our government and its elected officials continue to plummet? Will your streets and neighborhoods be safe? Will you want to live behind walled and gated communities? Change is often frightening and painful. It ushers in tremendous challenges, but it can also offer unprecedented opportunities. Will you be prepared to meet the challenges and seize the opportunities? Read on. This book tells you how to go through college and graduate ready for what's ahead.

■ Identifying the Computer Skills That You Need

What Is Your Level of Computer Literacy? What Are the Computer Skills You Will Need in Your Academic Program and in the Workplace?

Computer Skills needed to succeed in college:

- *Basic to intermediate operational skills*
- *Basic to intermediate keyboarding skills*
- *Basic to intermediate Internet skills*
- *Intermediate word processing skills*

As you progress through your first quarter at NEIT and the quarters to follow, computer skills will be identified for mastery. It is critical to your success as a student to establish your present level of computer competency. When such a baseline is established, you will be able to formulate a plan to get from your baseline to the level of the required computer skills.

The need to develop any specific skills, to learn software packages or programming languages depends entirely upon your program of study. The degree to which you need to develop these skills also depends upon the career you choose and the level at which you are hired. Well-developed computer skills will always be an asset to you and to your employer.

How Can the Academic Skills Center Help You to Improve Your Computer Skills?

In addition to the services mentioned in Chapter Three, the ASC also provides a number of services relating to computer skills. No appointment is necessary to use computers that have Internet access and a variety of software packages. The ASC also offers an enrichment course entitled Keyboarding to Surfing, a two-credit course which can help to strengthen computer skills.

The Academic Skills Center's Web Site

If you click on the Computer Services button at the ASC web site, you'll get access to all sorts of interesting information. Choices include the following:

- *Will I be arrested?* This link explains computer error messages and what they mean. It also provides some tips about what to do about those messages.
- *Tutorials* on keyboarding (including typing tutors), Windows 95 and 98, Microsoft Office 97, how to repair a CD-ROM and using the Internet. Some of these tutorials are also available on CD-ROM in the ASC.
- *Tips and Tricks* has links that lead to a computer skills assessment test, a Microsoft Word quick reference sheet and a dictionary of computer terms.
- *Fun Sites* includes links to several fun quizzes, some computer-related jokes and several other fascinating sites.

■ Summary

- Being computer literate is essential to meeting the demands of the new millennium.
- The Academic Skills Center provides computers for student use and computer skill specialists to tutor you with specific computer software needs.
- The Academic Skills Center web site offers helpful tips, tools and course work which provides instruction in hardware, software and computer applications.

Additional Resources

Resources in the Learning Resources Center (call numbers are shown in parentheses after the citation):

Alliance for Technology Access. (1996). *Computer resources for people with disabilities: a guide to exploring today's assistive technology.* Alameda, CA: Hunter House Publishers. (HV1569.5 .C675 1996)

Mayo, D. & Berkemeyer, K. (1998). *Internet in an hour for beginners.* New York: DDC Pub. (TK5105.875 .I57 M371 1998)

Whitehead, P. & Maran, R. (1997). *Internet and World Wide Web simplified.* Foster City, CA: IDG Books Worldwide. (TK5105.875 .I57 W44 1997).

Web Sites:

Please note that web site addresses often change. If you are unable to reach the addresses below, use a search engine and search the source of the site or the title of the web document to find the new site.

This list includes some of the web sites that are listed at the Academic Skills Center's web page. For more sites (updated regularly), go to the ASC's web page.

Central Kansas Library System:
http://www.ckls.org/~crippel/computerlab/tutorials/index.html
CNet Internet Errors Explained:
http://coverage.cnet.com/Resources/Tech/Advisers/Error/
IVillage.com Clicktionary:
http://www.ivillage.com/click/tools/clicktionary/
IVillage.com Computer Tour:
http://www.ivillage.com/click/tools/computertour
ZDNet, "How to Buy a Computer":
http://www5.zdnet.com/zdhelp/stories/main/0,5594,363788,00.html

On-Campus Resources:

Academic Skills Center, Center for the Technologies, Third Floor, (401) 739-5000, Ext. 3416.

Activities

5-1   Complete the Computer Skills Assessment Chart (in the Appendix, p. 168) and rate your level of skill on each of the computer skills identified in your group work. Place it in your Career Inventory Folder. (You can complete a more in-depth online computer skills assessment at the Academic Skills Center's web site.)

5-2   Access the Academic Skills Center web site and identify where you can go and what services you can use to improve your skill level.

CHAPTER 6
Acquiring Career Information
Via the World Wide Web

*"My life was turned upside down when I had to make a career change due to a disability.
I was 42 with no useful job skills. I didn't know a proton from an electron, and the last time
I had been in an algebra class prior to NEIT was when Nixon was president. Despite all of
this, I enrolled in the Electronics Technology program. I will, for the rest of my life, be
thankful for the teachers I had at NEIT. Every one of them explained things in a way that
someone with no technical experience could understand. Today, I am employed in a great job
at EMC Corporation. I really feel that New England Tech changed my life."*

Michael Dwyer
Electronics Technology

Chapter Designers:

Sharon J. Charette, Learning Resources Center Director
David J. Cranmer, Associate Professor of Humanities and Social Science
Thomas R. Thibodeau, Director of the Center for Distributed Learning

What Students Are Saying . . .

"My experience with TEC 101 has been a positive one. Even though I have been using a computer for several years now, I found that this course has helped me in an area in which my skills were weak, the use of the Internet for research. I enjoyed the class on this area and was able to use this new knowledge in my other classes that required several research papers."

Gordon Tempest
Computer Networking and Servicing Technology

In This Chapter

You will become familiar with and be able to describe

- The differences between the World Wide Web and the Internet.
- The role of a browser.

You will learn how to use your browser to access useful web sites on the World Wide Web (WWW).

■ Introduction

Being comfortable with using the Internet for work and for personal use is becoming increasingly important. This chapter will introduce you to part of the Internet—the World Wide Web. You will explore a variety of career-related web sites and search for job descriptions specific to your technology. By examining job descriptions, you can see the importance of many of the skills and concepts that will be introduced in your technical courses.

■ What Is the Internet?

The Internet was started in the late 1960s as a network of computers for use by research scientists, academic institutions and the military. It has since grown to become a massive network of computers connected together for the purpose of research, education, communication and recreation. Now, the Internet is as common as the telephone and television—and as indispensable. People from all walks of life in countries all around the world routinely use the Internet as part of their everyday life.

■ What Is the World Wide Web?

The World Wide Web is just one part of the Internet. It comprises locations referred to as web sites which are made up of files called web pages which can deliver text, video images, audio files and pictures to your desktop. A web site is a collection of web pages. Currently over 800 million web pages are registered with the World Wide Web. Web pages are written in a computer language called "hypertext mark-up language," abbreviated as HTML.

Why Use the World Wide Web?

There are many reasons why the World Wide Web is important for research today. The World Wide Web is made up of web sites that can provide

- *the most current information on news events, weather, sports*

- *the most recent scientific findings*

- *current survey results*

- *complete reports that are often too long for newspapers or magazines to print in full*

- *access to information located far away from your local library or your home*

- *directories, telephone books, maps and all sorts of reference materials that are updated frequently*

- *the latest revisions to existing laws, regulations and codes*

Getting to the World Wide Web

There are three things that you need to get to the World Wide Web. First, you need a computer. Next, you need an Internet service provider which provides the connection between your computer and the WWW via a telephone or cable line. Finally, you need a browser (sometimes called a web browser), which is a computer program that allows you to access web pages by typing in an address.

Computer

In order to get to the World Wide Web you obviously need a computer. While many computers can give you access to the web, it is important to bear a few things in mind before you go out to make a purchase. Web access—or any computer use for that matter—is more productive and more pleasant if you have a computer with as much capability as you can afford.

The following items should be examined while purchasing a computer: processor speed, RAM (random access memory), modem speed and multimedia capability (sound and video). The processor and modem speeds and RAM help to provide quick access to the web. Multimedia capabilities allow you to fully explore web sites that have sound and video clips. A printer is also necessary so that you can print out any of the information that you find on the web.

What You Need for Internet Access

1. *Computer with a Modem*
2. *Internet Service Provider*
3. *Web Browser*

Internet Service Provider

An Internet Service Provider (ISP) is necessary to get access to the World Wide Web. Some are free and some charge a variety of fees for the type of access that they offer. Service can be provided through a telephone line or cable connection. Though a cable connection provides the quickest Internet service, it is currently the most expensive.

When selecting an ISP, you need to consider the following things:

- speed of connection—be sure that the provider you choose can accommodate the highest speed of your modem.
- reliability—choose a reliable ISP. Ask them how many lines they have and what their refusal percentage is. Also ask people you know which provider they use and if they are pleased with the access and service.
- cost—check on the monthly cost and check to see if there are local telephone numbers that you can dial into without incurring toll charges.
- number of hours of access provided in the plan—if you use over the number of hours provided for in your plan, you will incur additional charges.
- availability of technical support—technical support is often unavailable with free service providers.

Internet service providers include some nationally-known companies like AOL, Prodigy, CompuServe and MSN that charge a monthly fee, local Internet service providers and cable companies, who charge a monthly fee; and a growing number of free providers (such as NetZero.com, AltaVista). Those that charge a monthly fee also provide other services in addition to access to the World Wide Web. Service plans are priced according to how many hours you plan to connect to the Internet and if you exceed your time limit, per-hour charges are incurred.

What About Free Internet Service Providers?

More and more free Internet service providers are cropping up offering connection to the Internet with no monthly fee. Many of these services are worth looking into in order to save some money. How can they offer the service for free? Many of these feature an advertising display which cannot be removed from the screen. The revenues from this advertising subsidize the cost of the service. In addition, some of these services conduct frequent surveys of subscribers or monitor the web sites that you visit and collect that information to provide to advertisers. Free Internet service providers are often as reliable as those for which you have to pay. In order to ensure reliable access all the time, it's not a bad idea to sign up with more than one free Internet service provider. This will give you a backup in case there are problems with one of the providers. How do you get to one of these free providers if you don't already have Internet access? You can search for them on the Internet at a public access computer at your college or local public library. Many of them provide a telephone number that you can call to order a disk by mail.

Web Browser

A browser is a computer program which allows you to gain access to the web. The two most widely used web browsers are Netscape Navigator and Microsoft Internet Explorer. A browser locates the web site or web page you want from the web address that you type into the box at the top of the screen.

Much like the address that you would write on an envelope to deliver a piece of mail to a specific address, a Uniform Resource Locator (or URL) is entered in the browser's "address" or "go to" box to enable you to contact the web address that you need. URLs typically begin with http://. There is no final period at the end of a URL. Between the beginning and ending are other parts of the URL which identify the organization hosting the web site/web page as well as the "domain" within the Internet where the organization is registered. While words are most commonly used in URLs for business and organizations, numbers are also used. URLs that consist primarily of numbers are Internet protocol (IP) addresses—the actual numerical address of a web site.

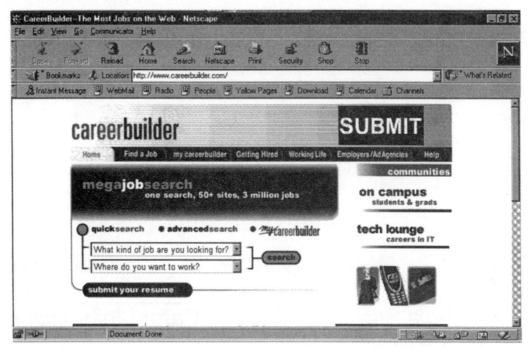

Netscape Communicator

Comparison of Netscape Communicator and Microsoft Internet Explorer screens.

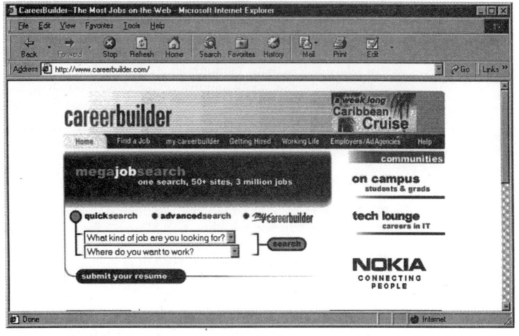

Microsoft Internet Explorer

Domain names refer to geographical divisions (such as state and country names) as well as to categories of organizations. These domain names often provide useful clues about the origin of the information provided at the web site.

Domain Names

Domain names identify the source of information at a web site. The most common domain names are:

        .com *for commercial organizations*

        .edu *for educational institutions*

        .gov *for federal government organizations*

        .mil *for military organizations*

        .net *for Internet organizations*

        .org *for non-profit organizations*

■ Using a Browser to Acquire Career Information on the WWW

The web can be a valuable source of career information. You can easily find electronic "want ads" which provide detailed job descriptions, including lists of the skills that you'll need to obtain a good job. The web sites in the following chart include a wide variety of career-oriented web sites. You can use these URLs to search for career information, for tips on how to write a resume and for how to prepare for an interview. You may also want to consult the *Occupational Outlook Handbook* (http://www.bls.gov) which provides information on careers, including educational requirements, skills, job outlook and potential salary. The web sites of professional organizations and many company-sponsored web sites also provide useful information for career research.

■ Summary

- ■ The World Wide Web (WWW) comprises electronic documents networked together for public access.
- ■ A browser enables you to access electronic documents on the World Wide Web.
- ■ Documents are accessed through addresses called Uniform Resource Locators (URLs).
- ■ The Web delivers a world of current information from many sources directly to your desktop.

Additional Resources

Resources in the Learning Resources Center (call numbers are shown in parentheses after the citation):

ActiveEducation. (1999). *Microsoft Internet Explorer 5 step by step.* Redmond, WA: Microsoft Press. (TK5105.883 .M53 M5356 1999)

Calishain, T. & Nystrom, J. A. (1998). *Official Netscape guide to Internet research: for Windows & Macintosh.* Scottsdale, AZ: Coriolis Group. (TK5105.883 .N48 C35 1998)

Dikel, M. F. & Roehm, F. E. (2000). *The guide to Internet job searching.* Lincolnwood, (Chicago), IL: VGM Career Horizons. (Career Planning HF5382.7 .R557 2000)

Frew, J. , Mayo, D., & Berkemeyer, K. (1998). *Internet in an hour for students.* New York: DDC Pub. (TK5105.875 .I57 F73 1998)

Hoffman, P. (1996). *Netscape and the World Wide Web for dummies.* Foster City, CA: IDG Books Worldwide. (TK5105.883 .N48 1996)

Jandt, F. E. & Nemnich, M. B. (1997). *Using the Internet and the World Wide Web in your job search.* Indianapolis, IN: JIST Works. (Career Planning HF5382.7 .J36 1997)

Mayo, D. & Berkemeyer, K. (1998). *Internet in an hour for beginners.* New York: DDC Pub. (TK5105.875 .I57 M371 1998)

Nelson, S. L. (1996). *The World Wide Web for busy people.* Berkeley, CA: Osborne/ McGraw-Hill. (TK5105.888 .N35 1996)

Nemnich, M. B. & Jandt, F. E. (2000). *Cyberspace job search kit.* Indianapolis, IN: JIST Works. (Career Planning HF5382.7 .N448 2000)

Ray, E. J., Ray, D. S. & Seltzer, R. (1998). *The AltaVista search revolution.* Berkeley, CA: Osborne/McGraw-Hill. (TK5105.883 .A48 R29 1998)

Whitehead, P. & Maran, R. (1997). *Internet and World Wide Web simplified.* Foster City, CA: IDG Books Worldwide. (TK5105.875 .I57 W44 1997).

Web Sites:

Please note that web site addresses often change. If you are unable to reach the addresses below, use a search engine and search the source of the site or the title of the web document to find the new site.

NetZero: http://www.netzero.com
Occupational Outlook Handbook: http://www.bls.gov

Career Related Web Sites
America's Job Bank: http://www.ajb.dni.us/
Black Enterprise Career Channel:
    http://findjob.blackenterprise.com/52/pageopen.asp?source=pages/ careerstab.htm
Bloomberg: http://www.bloomberg.com/careers/index.html?sidenav=front
Boston Globe Career Path: http://careerpath.boston.com/
Brass Ring.com: http://www.jobcenter.com/
Business Week Online Career Center:
    http://findjob.businessweek.com/careers/index.html
Career Builder: http://careerbuilder.com
Career City: http://www.careercity.com/
Career.com: http://www.career.com/
CareerExchange: http://www.careerexchange.com/
Career Magazine: http://www.careermag.com/

CareerWeb: http://www.cweb.com
Catapult: http://www.jobweb.org/catapult/catapult.htm
Changing Channels: http://www.channels.org/links/index.html
City Search: http://citysearch.com
College Central: http://www.collegecentral.com/
College Grad Job Hunter: http://www.collegegrad.com/
ComputerWork.com: http://www.computerwork.com/
DICE: http://www.dice.com/
e-inSITE.net: http://www.e-inSITE.net/e-insite/FindJob.asp
FlipDog.com: http://www.flipdog.com/
Get A Job: http://www.getajob.com
Good Works: http://www.essential.org/goodworks/
Head Hunter: http://www.headhunter.net/
Hispanic Online Cyber Career Center: http://findjob.hisp.com/
HotJobs: http://www.hotjobs.com/
Itcareers.com: http://ITcareers.com
ITClassifieds.com: http://www.ITClassifieds.com/
JobBankUSA: http://www.jobbankusa.com/
jobfind.com: http://www.jobfind.com
Job Hunter's Bible: http://www.JobHuntersBible.com
Job-Hunt: http://www.job-hunt.org/jobs-all/shtml
JobOptions:
    http://www.joboptions.com/esp/plsql/espan_enter.espan_home
jobs.Internet.com: http://jobs.Internet.com
Jobs4IT: http://www.jobs4it.com/
JobSmart: http://www.jobsmart.org
Jobweb: http://www.jobweb.com/
Media Central: http://www.mediacentral.com/careers/
Monster.com: http://Monster.com
MSN Careers: http://careers.msn.com/
NationJob: http://www.nationjob.com/
OmniOne Recruitment: http://www.omnione.com/careeropps.html
Preferred Jobs: http://www.preferredjobs.com/
Providence Journal Classifieds: http://careers.projo.com/
QuestLink Career Circuit: http://careers.questlink.com/
Riley Guide: http://www.dbm.com/jobguide
SelectJobs: http://www.selectjobs.com/
Softwarejobs.com: http://www.softwarejobs.com/
TelecomWeb Career Center: http://www.telecomweb.com/telecomjobs/
The Job Resource: http://www.jobresource.com/
USA Today: http://bestjobsusa.com
WETA CareerCenter: http://www.weta.org/careers/content.html
World Wide Web Employment Office: http://www.employmentoffice.net/

On-Campus Resources:

Academic Skills Center, Center for the Technologies, Third Floor, (401) 739-5000, Ext. 3416.

Learning Resources Center, Corner of Post Road and Baywood Street, (401) 739-5000, Ext. 3409.

Activities

6-1   Print out any relevant information from the web sites on the previous pages that
      can help you answer your career exploration questions.

6-2   Use the *Occupational Outlook Handbook* (http://www.bls.gov) to fill in your Skills
      Self-Assessment form.

6-3   If you wish to find more information related to your career goals, use the com-
      puter to access one or more of the web sites in a *Subject Resource Series* booklet
      appropriate to your technology.

Name: _____ Date: _____

Activity 6-2. Skills Self-Assessment Form

In the first column, list the skills that you have identified as necessary in your field. In the second column, rate your current level of skill on a scale of 1 to 5 (1 = no skill, 2 = little skill, 3 = moderate skill, 4 = good skill level, 5 = expert level skill). In the third column, check the skills that you need to develop.

Skill	Current Level of This Skill	Need To Develop This Skill
Technical Skills		
Supporting Skills		

CHAPTER 7
Using Search Engines

"When my company closed, I had been there for 11 years and thought I would retire there. Without an education, I knew I wouldn't have a good future. So despite the anxiety of returning to school after a 15-year absence, I enrolled in the Administrative Medical Assistant Technology program. I received a lot of personal attention from the faculty and threw myself into my studies. All of my hard work paid off; I am now employed as an ophthalmic technician with a local eye surgeon."

Christine Cahoon
Administrative Medical Assistant Technology

Chapter Designers:

Sharon J. Charette, Learning Resources Center Director
David J. Cranmer, Associate Professor of Humanities and Social Science
Thomas R. Thibodeau, Director of the Center for Distributed Learning

What Students Are Saying . . .

"Besides all the background and support service information, we were given an opportunity to use computers to both assess our skills and find information on our technology. I was able to look up information on hardware and job information for computer networking through some of the job sites and search engines."

Tom Butts
Computer and Network Servicing Technology

In This Chapter

You will become familiar with search engines and what they do.

You will learn how to

- ■ Search the World Wide Web.
- ■ Enhance your searching skills by using the appropriate search engine and effective search strategies.
- ■ Evaluate information found on the World Wide Web.

■ Introduction

T he World Wide Web comprises over 800 million web pages. With such a large amount of material available, it is important to develop strategies that will enable you to quickly retrieve the exact information that you need. search engines enable you to locate the information that you seek.

This chapter will teach you some of the techniques of using search engines and will acquaint you with several of the most widely used search engines. Not all search engines are equal—you need different search engines to locate different kinds of information.

■ The Role of a Search Engine

You may wonder why you need a search engine if you already have a browser that gets you to web pages. Just like when you use a library, you may not know the title or location of a book that has the information that you need, but you would know the subject that you are interested in. A search engine helps you to find the web pages which might contain information on a subject that you are looking for when you don't know the URL.

A search engine is a computer program that lets you identify some subject terms to find web pages from the Internet that contain those terms. If you have chosen good search terms, then the search engine will show you only pages that have the information you are looking for. Using a search engine speeds up the process of locating what you need by sifting through millions of web pages and returning only items that relate directly to the terms that you used for your search.

Why Use More than One Search Engine?

There are two major reasons for using more than one search engine. For one thing, each search engine covers only a small portion of the World Wide Web. Each web site must register with search engines and most web sites do not register with all search engines. So if you use only one search engine, you may miss web sites that will be helpful to you.

A second reason for having more than one search engine is that each search engine uses its own method of searching for information. Depending on the kind of material you are looking for, one search engine might have a better method than other search engines.

In addition to standard search engines, there are also meta search engines which search the results of multiple search engines. These can be useful when you want to get an overall view of the information that is available on a particular topic or when you are having difficulty finding information using a standard search engine. When using a meta search engine, be sure to select one or two simple terms or few results will be returned.

The following tutorials contain more information about the World Wide Web, search engines and search strategies. Don't hesitate to revisit these tutorials to refresh your memory about search engines.

- "Finding Information on the Web"
  http://www.lib.berkeley.edu/TeachingLib/Guides/Internet/FindInfo.html

OR

- "Bare Bones 101: A Basic Tutorial on Searching the Web"
  http://www.sc.edu/beaufort/library/bones.html

How to Search the World Wide Web

One of the best ways to start getting used to searching is to access a search engine and type in several sample searches. This will give you an idea of what kind and how much information is available. After a bit of practice, you can see that adding multiple terms or using some of the tips listed later on in this chapter can greatly improve the accuracy of your searches.

You can also improve your searching by using the tutorials and search tips included at the web site of each search engine. If you spend time improving your search skills now, you will save a lot of time in the future sifting through hundreds of documents to find the one that answers your question.

Search Engines Recommended for College-level Courses

- Alta Vista: http://www.altavista.com/
- Excite: http://www.excite.com/
- Fast Search: http://www.ussc.alltheweb.com/
- Google: http://www.google.com/
- HotBot: http://www.hotbot.com/
- Northern Light: http://www.northernlight.com/
- Yahoo!: http://www.yahoo.com/

In order to access a search engine, you enter its URL in the "go to" or "address" box at the top of your Internet browser screen. Type in the address and then press the ENTER key. After you have accessed the search engine, you will see a box at the top of the screen that will allow you to type in a search term. At the end of that box is usually a button that says "find" or "search."

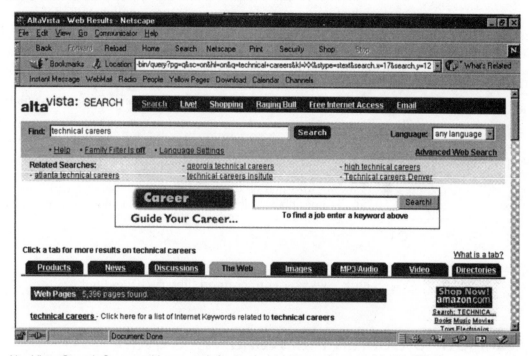

Alta Vista Search Screen with a search for "technical careers" entered in the *Find* box.

After your search has been completed, you will see a results list on the screen. Please note that key information in each of these items on the list is underlined and is blue. These are called "hyperlinks." Clicking on these links will get you to the information in the results list.

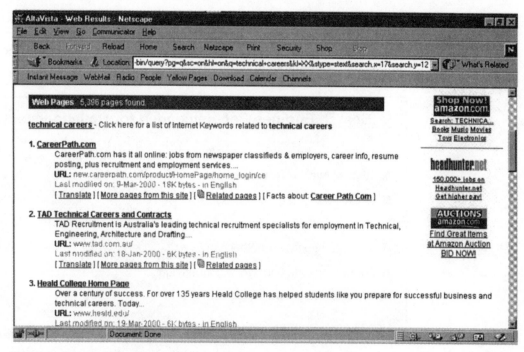

Alta Vista Results List with Hyperlinks

When you encounter a hyperlink within any of these web sites, clicking on it will get you to additional information about the text that is highlighted in blue or to other web sites mentioned in the text. Hyperlinks are a useful way of linking to other information on topics that you are interested in researching.

Tips for Finding Information Using Search Engines

Please remember the following tips when using a search engine:

- Spelling counts—a misspelled word will not retrieve much information.
- Be specific when entering search terms—very broad terms like "psychology" will return far too many hits to be useful. Using several more specific terms will help you find the information you need.
- *But . . .* don't be too specific—an extremely narrow search which includes too many words is not likely to pull up the information that you need.
- *Do* use some of the search tips that are provided on each search engine's web site. They teach some effective strategies for getting the information you need more quickly and efficiently. Some of those strategies are illustrated on the chart shown on the next page.
- If you are using one search engine and cannot find what you are looking for, try a few others.
- If you still cannot find anything, try using one of the meta search engines (such as The Big Hub, Dogpile, Inference Find or MetaCrawler) with a broader term.

The Search Engine Features chart on the next page shows some additional strategies for getting the most out of your searches. By combining terms in quotation marks, by requiring that words be included or excluded and by using wildcard matches to retrieve all forms of a word, you can find the appropriate, useful information efficiently. This chart includes some information from each of these search engines' tutorials.

The chart below called Other Useful Search Engines, contains web addresses for some of the major meta search engines and a variety of additional search engines with specific subject focuses.

Evaluating Web Sites

Though web sites are a rich source of information, they can also pose some research problems. Since many web sites do not conform to the same sorts of verification or editorial review as print publications, it is important to know how you can evaluate the resources that you retrieve over the web. Several aspects of web sites or web documents can be used to judge the usefulness and authority of the information. The web document entitled "Evaluating Information Found on the Internet" by Elizabeth E. Kirk (http://milton.mse.jhu.edu:8001/research /education/net.html) includes more detailed information about some of the points listed below as well as several additional points.

Search Engine Features

Web Address	Alta Vista www.altavista.com	Fast Search www.alltheweb.com	Northern Light www.northernlight.com	Excite www.excite.com	HotBot www.hotbot.com	Yahoo! www.yahoo.com
Search for Exact Phrases "*state of the union*"	put words in double quotation marks ("")	put words in double quotation marks ("") and click on all of the words in the drop down menu	put words in double quotation marks ("")	put words in double quotation marks ("") or use Advanced Web Search and select *MUST contain the word(s)*	put words in double quotation marks ("") or select *exact phrase* from the Look For pull-down menu	put words in double quotation marks ("")
Word/Phrase must be included in result *snake +python*	use plus sign (+) before the word	use plus sign (+) before the word	use plus sign (+) before the word	use Advanced Web Search and select *MUST contain* from the pull-down menu	use plus sign (+) before the word	use plus sign (+) before the word
Word/Phrase must **not** be included in result *+python -monty*	use minus sign (–) before the word	use minus sign (–) before the word	use minus sign (–) before the word	use Advanced Web Search and select *MUST NOT contain* from the pull-down menu	use minus sign (–) before the word	use minus sign (–) before the word
Wildcard matching—to include all forms of a word ***medic**** (for medic, medicine, medical, medicinal, etc.)	Use an asterisk (*) to retrieve all forms of the search term		use an asterisk (*) to retrieve all forms of the search term	automatic	use an asterisk (*) to retrieve all forms of the search term	use an asterisk (*) to retrieve all forms of the search term
Is there a simple search for Audio, Video, or Images?	click on Images, Audio & Video tab	click on Picture Search or Listening Room		click on Advanced Audio Video Search	click on boxes at the left side of the search screen	

Other Useful Search Engines		
Search Engine Name	**URL/Web Address**	**Features**
AlphaSearch	http://www.calvin.edu/Library/searreso/Internet/as/	searches academic sites
Ask Jeeves	http://www.askjeeves.com	good for trivia
The Big Hub	http://www.thebighub.com	searches multiple search engines
BUBL Link	http://www.bubl.ac.uk/link	for academic users
Dogpile	http://www.dogpile.com	searches multiple search engines
FindLaw	http://www.findlaw.com	searches legal web sites
Go Network	http://infoseek.go.com	standard search engine
Google	http://www.google.com	standard search engine that displays results based on popularity of sites with other users
Infomine	http://infomine.ucr.edu	searches academic sites
MapQuest	http://www.mapquest.com	maps, driving directions and local information (restaurants, hotels)
MetaCrawler	http://www.metacrawler.com	searches multiple search engines
Oingo	http://www.oingo.com	helps you refine your search by giving you choices for the meanings of the search terms
Yahoo! People Search	http://people.yahoo.com/	searches telephone directories to find telephone numbers, addresses and e-mail addresses

What to Look for When Evaluating a Web Site

■ Domain Name/Point of view
The domain name (.com—commercial, .org—organization, .mil—military, .gov—government, .edu—education) can give you a good idea of the point of view of the author of the information located on the web site. Depending on the type of information that you need, all of these serve a very good purpose. If you need to find technical specifications or information on a specific product, then a commercial web site is probably your best bet. If you need to find unbiased research on a topic, you'll probably do better at an .edu web site. Web sites of organizations, the military and the government provide useful information but they do also have a specific bias or point of view. As Kirk cautions in the web document mentioned above, "information is rarely neutral." You should always be very aware of who is presenting the information and what their bias might be.

■ Author/Publishing body
Check to see if the author or publishing organization of the information in a web site is named. Sometimes you will be able to check on the author or publisher's credentials by looking up the name on the World Wide Web. The information included in a web site can be judged as more legitimate if the author's name is listed,

if there is some biographical information, or if the author's address, telephone number or e-mail address are listed. By providing a means of researching and contacting an author, the author is indicating that they are willing to take responsibility for the information they have presented.

◼ Last date updated
To determine how current the information is, check at the end of the web document. Usually, there is a date listed at the end of the document that indicates when the last update was done or when the document was first published electronically.

Armed with all of the pointers presented in this chapter, you will be able to find the information that you need for your courses and for your personal needs.

◼ Summary

◼ Search engines can help you find information on subjects that interest you.
◼ Each search engine accesses a different set of web sites and has its own method of locating and ranking the web sites that are found as a result of your search.
◼ Each search engine provides a tutorial telling you how to get the best results with that search engine.
◼ In addition, there are other web sites that offer general tutorials on how to construct the most productive searches for information on the WWW.
◼ Hyperlinks can help you to get to additional information on the topics that you have searched.
◼ The domain name, the point of view, the author and the last date updated can help you judge the reliability of information found on the World Wide Web.

Additional Resources

Resources in the Learning Resources Center (call numbers are shown in parentheses after the citation):

ActiveEducation. (1999). *Microsoft Internet Explorer 5 step by step*. Redmond, WA: Microsoft Press. (TK5105.883 .M53 M5356 1999)

Calishain, T. & Nystrom, J. A. (1998). *Official Netscape guide to Internet research: for Windows & Macintosh*. Scottsdale, AZ: Coriolis Group. (TK5105.883 .N48 C35 1998)

Dikel, M. F. & Roehm, S. O. (1998). *The guide to Internet job searching*. Lincolnwood, (Chicago), IL: VGM Career Horizons. (Career Planning HF5382.7 .R557 1998)

Frew, J. , Mayo, D., & Berkemeyer, K. (1998). *Internet in an hour for students*. New York: DDC Pub. (TK5105.875 .I5 F73 1998)

Glossbrenner, A. & Glossbrenner, E. (1998). *Search engines for the World Wide Web*. Berkeley, CA: Peachpit Press. (Ref. TK5105.888 .G57 1998)

Gould, C. (1998). *Searching smart on the World Wide Web: tools and techniques for getting quality results*. Berkeley, CA: Library Solutions Press. (TK5105.888 .G68 1998)

Hock, R. (1999). *The extreme searcher's guide to web search engines: a handbook for the serious searcher*. Medford, NJ: CyberAge Books. (ZA4226 .H63 1999)

Hoffman, P. (1996). *Netscape and the World Wide Web for dummies*. Foster City, CA: IDG Books Worldwide. (TK5105.883 .N48 1996)

Jandt, F. E. & Nemnich, M. B. (1997). *Using the Internet and the World Wide Web in your job search*. Indianapolis, IN: JIST Works. (Career Planning HF5382.7 .J36 1997)

Ray, E. J., Ray, D. S. & Seltzer, R. (1998). *The AltaVista search revolution*. Berkeley, CA: Osborne/McGraw-Hill. (TK5105.883 .A48 R29 1998)

Whitehead, P. & Maran, R. (1997). *Internet and World Wide Web simplified*. Foster City, CA: IDG Books Worldwide. (TK5105.875 .I57 W44 1997).

Web Sites:

Please note that web site addresses often change. If you are unable to reach the addresses below, use a search engine and search the source of the site or the title of the web document to find the new site.

Evaluating Web Sites

Widener University, Wolfgram Memorial library: http://www2.widener.edu/Wolfgram-Memorial-Library/webevaluation/webeval.htm and for information about evaluating web resources with specific domain names (.com, .org, .edu, .gov), click on this web site http://www2.widener.edu/Wolfgram-Memorial-Library/ and follow the links at the bottom of the screen.

Johns Hopkins University, Milton S. Eisenhower Library: http://milton.mse.jhu.edu:8001/research/education/net.html

Montgomery County Public Schools, Rockville, MD, "Critical Evaluation of a World Wide Web Site": http://www.mcps.k12.md.us/schools/springbrookhs/webeval.html

Search Engines

Alta Vista: http://www.altavista.com/

Excite: http://www.excite.com/

Fast Search: http://www.ussc.alltheweb.com/

Google: http://www.google.com

HotBot: http://www.hotbot.com/

Northern Light: http://www.northernlight.com/

Yahoo!: http://www.yahoo.com/

Tutorials

University of California, Berkeley Library, "Finding Information on the Web": http://www.lib.berkeley.edu /TeachingLib/Guides/Internet/FindInfo.html

University of South Carolina, Beaufort Library, "Bare Bones 101: A Basic Tutorial on Searching the Web": http://www.sc.edu/beaufort/library/bones.html

On-Campus Resources:

Academic Skills Center, Center for the Technologies, Third Floor, (401) 739-5000, Ext. 3416.

Learning Resources Center, Corner of Post Road and Baywood Street, (401) 739-5000, Ext. 3409.

Activities

7-1   Use search engines to find information that may answer some of your career exploration questions.

7-2   Access a web site from the *Subject Resource Series* booklet(s) appropriate to your technology. Examine the web site and look for the elements listed above (domain name, author, point of view and last date updated).

Optional Activities

■ *Work through the following web sites which are recommended to help you learn to evaluate web sites.*

1. *Evaluating Web Resources: http://www2.widener.edu/ Wolfgram-Memorial-Library/webevaluation/webeval.htm*

2. *Evaluating Information Found on the Internet: http://milton.mse.jhu.edu:8001/research/education/net.html*

■ *Evaluate two of the web sites that you visited in the previous lab activity (when you conducted a search of web sites relevant to your career exploration).*

Activity 7-2. Web Site Information

This chart can help you assess the information found on the sites you use in exploring your career questions.

Web Address (URL)	Domain Name/Point of View	Author/ Publishing Body	Last Date Updated

CHAPTER 8
Accessing and Evaluating Information

"I am the third generation in my family to attend New England Tech. My grandfather graduated in 1946 and my father finished in 1970. I currently work for my father's oil company; however, my family still wanted me to get a formal education and to receive training beyond what I receive on the job. My experience at NEIT has been great, and with the training I received, I plan to one day expand my family's business to include plumbing services."

Peter Cyr
Plumbing and Heating Technology

Chapter Designers:

Sharon J. Charette, Learning Resources Center Director
David J. Cranmer, Associate Professor of Humanities and Social Science

What Students Are Saying . . .

"The overview of the Learning Resources Center was extremely beneficial and again without this class I don't know if I would have learned about it on my own. In all honesty probably not. It was fascinating to learn what research is now available and how easy it is to gain access to it. Sure wish they had this when I first went to college 25 years ago."

Keith Maynard
Computer Information Systems Technology

In This Chapter

You will learn how to:

- Use the NEIT Learning Resources Center.
- Acquire and evaluate information.

■ Introduction

Developing research skills and learning how to find your way around a library are important parts to being successful in college and beyond. This chapter will help you to improve your research skills and develop new ones. It will include searching the online catalog, using EBSCOhost to obtain periodical articles, using the Internet to find information and evaluating Information from different sources. Learning the basics about how to locate and evaluate information are skills that you can use here at New England Tech's Learning Resources Center (library), at other libraries—and even at home.

The Learning Resources Center at New England Institute of Technology contains a wide variety of print, media and electronic resources chosen specifically to support the courses that you will take during your college career. Some of the resources offered can also be accessed from your home if you own a computer with a modem and an Internet service provider.

■ Research Skills

There are many ways to obtain information which can be presented in many different ways. Not very long ago, libraries only had print materials such as books and periodicals and bulky print sources such as card catalogs and indexes to organize and locate information. Now, electronic sources are used to get the full benefit of all the information available today. Using a combination of books, periodicals and Internet sources will allow you to get all the research materials you need to complete your course work.

The Impact of Gathering Information Electronically

There are many benefits to gathering information electronically:

- Speed: Depending upon your computer skills and the speed of your Internet access, a wealth of information can be gathered in minutes.
- Currency: Many web sites—especially those of news sources—are updated frequently (some hourly) each day. For instance, web sites such as MSNBC

(www.msnbc.com), local television stations and local newspapers update their sites frequently throughout the day and instantly when there is an important news story taking place.

U se a combination of books, periodicals and Internet sources to get all the information you need.

- A wealth of information at your desktop: From any computer that has Internet access, you can obtain information and print it out without leaving your desk. You can search web sites around the country and around the world for the information that you need.
- Low cost: With the wide availability of free Internet service providers, access to the Internet can be very inexpensive and reliable.

BUT, there are also a few drawbacks:

- Need good search skills: Without good search skills, locating the right information can sometimes be a time-consuming, frustrating task. Some of the tips from the previous chapter and from this chapter will help you find what you need much more efficiently.
- Source and dependability of information is difficult to determine: Since the World Wide Web is an unregulated and unrestricted resource, anybody from anywhere can create a web site and provide information that may *look* reliable when it is not. Refer back to the *Evaluating Web Sites* section of the previous chapter for ways to assess the source and reliability of information on web sites.
- Access can sometimes be slow: If you have a slow modem or an overly busy Internet Service Provider (ISP), sometimes searching and retrieving information can be painfully slow.

Because of the complexity and almost limitless amount of information available today, it is very important to learn some basic search skills. These would include using an online catalog, electronic periodical indexes and the Internet. The basic skills that you learn in this chapter can be used in any library or at any computer, though there may be some variations depending on the resources available.

It is important to be aware of the wealth of resources that are available to you and what the benefits of each are for obtaining the information that you need in college and throughout life. The three major resources that can be used to obtain information are books, periodicals and the World Wide Web. Each of these plays an important part in research and each has a variety of advantages and disadvantages, depending upon the type of research you are conducting.

Why Use the World Wide Web?

The World Wide Web provides the most current source of information, often updated daily—sometimes hourly. If you need information about anything that has happened within the past week or so, the World Wide Web is the place to go. With the exception of newspapers or radio and television broadcasts, there is no other way to get up-to-the-minute facts. It's also relatively simple to compare news reports from a variety of sources and from different points of view. Because there is little limitation on space, some lengthy documents related to important events (such as the Unabomber's manifesto in 1995 or Ken Starr's investigative report in 1998) were published in their entirety on the World Wide Web. Usually, though, information is presented in a short, summarized fashion when compared to books and periodicals.

S elect your sources carefully and you'll get the most out of the resources that are available to you.

Though the World Wide Web can be seductive as a one-stop source for information, it can rarely be used as the only source if you are preparing a research paper. As mentioned earlier, it is sometimes difficult to determine the source for information on a web site. There are no rules or regulations that require the person who wrote a document to be an authority on the subject they are writing about or even to identify who they are. Unless the web site is sponsored by a particular organization or authoritative body, the information rarely has to go through the same kind of scrutiny necessary for print materials. The end of Chapter Seven provides more in-depth information on evaluating World Wide Web resources.

Why Use Periodicals?

Periodicals are less current than World Wide Web resources but are more carefully documented. The term "periodical" refers to any publication that is issued with some regularity throughout the year. The more specific terms **magazine** and **journal** can also be used, though magazine is normally used for more casual publications such as *People* and journal is most commonly used for scholarly publications such as *Journal of Personality*. Many types of periodicals are available in the Learning Resources Center. Resources include a variety of daily newspapers, weekly news magazines, as well as scholarly, technical and professional journals which are published monthly, bimonthly, or quarterly. Articles found in periodicals are good for up-to-date and fairly concise presentations of information.

Depending on the type of periodical that you use, the information included is documented in different ways. Information presented in periodicals always goes through an editorial board which will verify facts and insure that the information presented is checked and correct. Professional and technical journals are likely to include references or additional readings that support the facts presented or the claims made in an article. Authors are identified and their credentials are often published to provide proof of their authority on a particular topic.

Why Use Books?

Though books are the least current information sources, they are among the most thoroughly researched and documented sources. Publishing a book can take up to three years from initial concept to final publishing. Why is that so? When nonfiction books are published, there is a rigorous process of editing, verification, fact checking and documentation that occurs. In addition, books often include numerous other references, glossaries, tables of contents and indexes which enable you to find information more quickly in a single self-contained source. Because of the process involved, books are best for in-depth research where the accuracy and depth of the information is important. Books are also most likely to have authors who are true authorities on a topic.

How Do I Decide What Resources to Use?

The resources that you use should depend on the kind of information that you need. Remember that the most current information can be found on the World Wide Web, but it is often difficult to determine who put together the information and what their point of view or area of expertise is. Periodicals provide a relatively current source of more detailed information with more reliable source-checking and fact verification than documents on the World Wide Web. Books are the least current source to use, but often provide in-depth, well-documented research with reference to many other supporting sources.

Regardless of the type of research you are doing, it is important to know how current the information is in the publication that you are using. Always be sure to check the publication date of sources that you use so that they are appropriate to your research. A paper on cutting-edge technology should always include very current resources, but a paper on history may include references that are decades old. It is also important to be aware of the author's credentials. Check web pages, articles and books for information about the background of authors and their credibility to write about the topic you are researching. Select your sources carefully and you'll get the most out of the resources that are available to you.

Using the Online Catalog

Most libraries now have online catalogs which make the process of locating a book on a particular topic much easier because the author, title, subject and keywords can be searched simultaneously. The online catalog at the Learning Resources Center includes information for all books and media materials owned by New England Tech.

To search for a book in the LRC's online catalog, you click on the "online catalog" icon which will get you to a basic search screen. At that search screen, you'll see the following:

- Boxes that let you select whether or not you want to search Titles, Authors, Subjects, Notes—or all four.
- Buttons that let you select whether you want the results of your search to "begin with," "contain," "closely match the word(s)," "stem from," or "sound like" your search term.
- A box that lets you type in your search term.
- A SEARCH button that initiates your search.

The "defaults," or preselected items, are the selections for "subjects" and "contain." This is because when people search, they are normally looking for a book on a subject that contains a particular term.

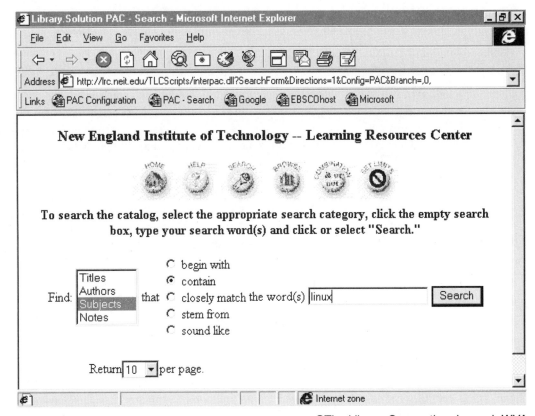

Search Screen

©The Library Corporation, Inwood, WVA

Please note that this process of searching is very similar to using a search engine to locate items on the World Wide Web. This is because the LRC's catalog is accessed through a web browser. Many of the skills that you learned by using a web browser and search engines will be of use to you in searching the online catalog.

After typing in a search term and clicking on the search button, the computer will return a list of all of the books and media materials that conform to this search. You'll also notice that all of the items in this list are highlighted in blue and underlined just as the hypertext links were highlighted and underlined on the World Wide Web. Just as with the WWW, clicking on any of these items will lead you to more detailed information or to another list from which to select other options.

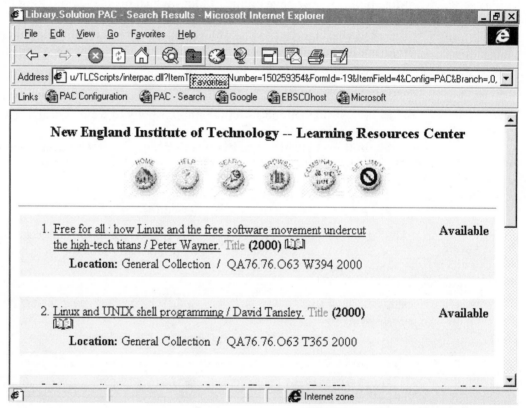

©The Library Corporation, Inwood, WVA

Titles that correspond to the search for subjects that contain "linux"

By clicking on the title "Free for all" you'll see a screen that contains all of the information that you need to locate the book and to list it properly on a term paper's "works cited" page. The illustration on the next page shows each of these elements in the display of one record in the online catalog.

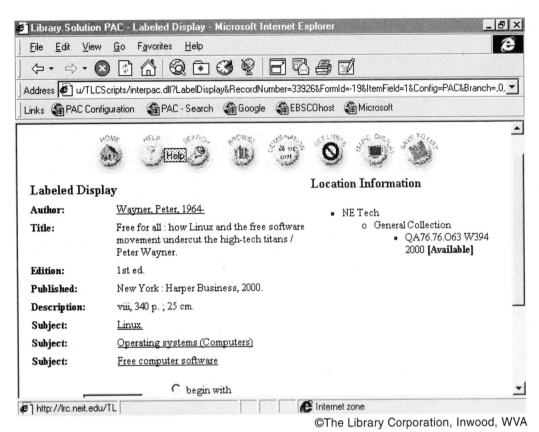

©The Library Corporation, Inwood, WVA

"Labeled Display" Screen of the Online Catalog

The bibliographic information on the screen includes all of the elements that describe a book. Most of this information will be needed when you create a "works cited" page for a research paper. Bibliographic information in the LRC's online catalog includes:

- Author: the primary person or organization that is responsible for creating the information in the book or the content of a media program—this may also include an editor
- Title: the title of the book
- Imprint: the city where the book was published, the name of the publisher and the date the information was published (this is important to check especially when you are looking for current materials)
- Description: physical description: the number of pages, height of the book in centimeters, whether or not there are illustrations and what type of illustrations are included, any accompanying materials (such as diskettes, charts, etc.)
- Subject headings: these are the topics that the book is mostly about
- Location: the collection the book is in (General Collection, Reference, Media, etc.), the call number (a series of letters and numbers that help you locate a book on the shelves) and availability (a note indicating if the item is available, checked out, overdue or lost)

Knowing what these items are and how to use them to get the information that you need will help you to do successful, efficient research. Following hypertext links to books on similar subjects or to books by the same author can help you get the most out of the LRC's collection. Once you learn how to use the LRC's online catalog, you will be able to use online catalogs in other libraries. Though there are many different vendors who produce online catalogs, most work in a similar manner.

The Library of Congress Classification System

Like most academic, research and special libraries, the LRC uses the Library of Congress Classification system. The *call number* is a series of letters and numbers that help you to locate the book on a library's shelves. This number appears in a straight line at the bottom of the online catalog screen and is typed on several lines on the book's spine label.

Each line of the call number on the spine label has a meaning. The example below illustrates that a great deal of information is represented in a call number. In the case of *Linux Application Development* by Johnson, this is what each set of numbers and letters mean:

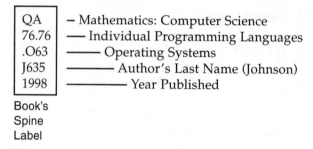

Call numbers are assigned to books so that the books on the same topic can be arranged together on the shelves. If you find a call number for a particular topic, you can be reasonably certain that other books on the same (or a very similar) topic will be located next to it.

Though most information on a topic will be shelved together in a collection, you do have to remember one thing. If you find multiple entries for a topic while searching the catalog, you should look at each of the entries to be sure that you have retrieved all the information you need. There are some topics that can be explored from different points of view that will appear in different parts of the collection. For example, books on the World Wide Web might be found in the TK classification for the networking aspects of the subject, in HD for e-commerce, in HG for online banking, in Z for creating a library home page and in PE for electronic communication. Though all of the books cover the topic of the World Wide Web, each explores the subject from a very different angle.

When selecting a book for research, please remember that it's important to make note of the date the book was published. If you are doing research on a topic relating to the humanities and social sciences or historical research on technology, you may want to use a combination of sources that are old and new. If you are doing technical research, you should use the most current sources available. Also, once you have located a book, it is also a good idea to check the table of contents and/or the index to determine if the book covers the aspect of the topic that you are interested in. Many books also contain information on the author's reputation or credentials in a particular field and a bibliography of other books on the same subject. All of these things will help you to determine the accuracy and depth of the book.

Finding Information in Periodicals

Finding information in periodicals is not very different from finding information on the World Wide Web or the online catalog. EBSCOhost is the primary tool used at New England Tech for finding relatively current articles in periodicals. This subscription service is also accessed using a web browser. EBSCOhost includes multiple databases that have indexing and abstracting for over 2000 periodicals and full-text/full-image for approxi-

Many electronic research tools such as online catalogs and online periodical databases use the same basic skills needed for using browsers and search engines.

mately 1000 of those titles (indexing/abstracts for most titles begins in the mid-1980s, full-text articles begin in the early 1990s). EBSCOhost is made up of *Academic Abstracts, Business Source Plus, Health Source Plus, ERIC* and several other reference works. These resources can be used together or separately. Many other libraries also subscribe to EBSCOhost or services that are very similar.

Some library terms need a bit of explanation. An **index** is used to look up an article by subject. Both print and electronic indexes speed up the time it takes to locate articles on a specific topic. Typically, print indexes cover several months to a year. Electronic indexes (like the one illustrated here) cover multiple years. An **abstract** is a description of the contents of an article. **Full-text** means that all of the words (text) of an article are included, but the illustrations are not. **Full-image** means that both the text and the illustrations are included in the database.

From the search screen, you have the option to limit searches by full-text, by magazine title or by date. To perform a keyword search, a term or terms can be typed in the box marked "Find." EBSCOhost's search engine will then search the text of articles and all elements of the entry (subject, title, abstract, etc.) for that term to produce a results list.

You can also do a subject search by clicking on the button in the EBSCOhost toolbar marked "Subject Search." This allows you to type in a term and select from a list of subjects based on that term. A subject search generally returns fewer—but more focused—results, since only the subjects assigned to the articles are searched. A subject search is often useful to refine your topic if you are researching a complicated subject that could be explored from a variety of angles.

Search Screen

When you type in a subject in the "Find" box and click on the SEARCH button in EBSCOhost, you will receive a list of articles that match your search term.

Note that this "Result List" below looks a bit like the screens you've seen on the WWW and in the online catalog. The top of the screen tells you how many articles have been retrieved (in this case 275) and displays the first 10 entries with the most recent article first. Each numbered entry includes (in this order): the title of the article, the title of the periodical, the date the article was published, the volume and issue, the page that the article is on and the total number of pages included in the article. This screen also lets you know if the LRC has the article or if the article is available in full-text right in the database. By quickly skimming this list, you can begin making an informed decision about which articles are most suitable for you based on the title, the length of the article and whether it is available in full text or is in the LRC.

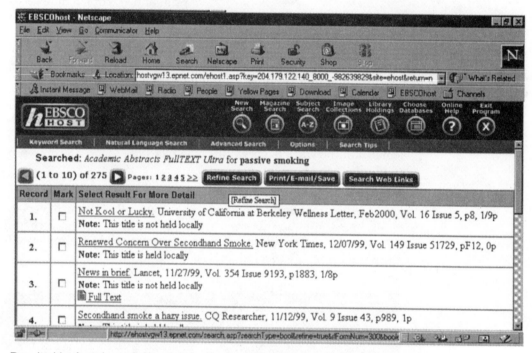

Results List for a keyword search for the term "passive smoking"

Clicking on the hyperlinks (blue underlined titles) brings you to the detailed information and, if available, the full text for each of these articles.

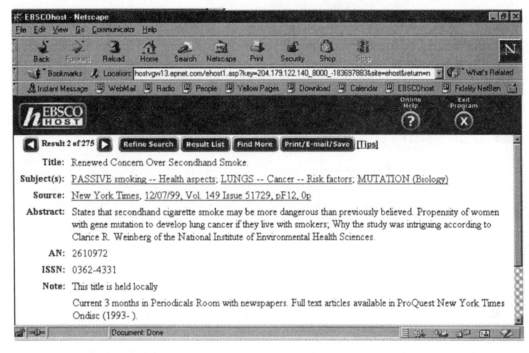

Detail Screen for One Article

As you can see in the illustration above, the detailed information for each article includes the following:

- The *title* of the article.
- Multiple *subjects* with hyperlinks to other articles on the same subject.
- The *source*, which includes the title of the periodical that the article appears in and detailed information about the *publishing date, volume, issue and page number* of the article as well as a description (number of pages, whether or not there are illustrations). The hyperlink for the periodical title leads you to a description of which contents are included in this database. Clicking on the date/issue hyperlink will lead you to a table of contents for that issue.
- The *author* of the article (if named).
- The *abstract*, or summary, of the contents of the article. You can save time by reading the abstracts before printing a full-text article or retrieving an article in paper copy on the shelves.
- *The AN*, or accession number assigned to the article by EBSCO.
- The *ISSN* is the international standard serial number assigned to each periodical title. This number is needed if you need to get an article through interlibrary loan.
- The *note* tells you whether or not the LRC owns that periodical and, if it does, where it is located.

If the article is included in full-text in the database, it can be found by scrolling down on the screen.

Clearly, if the article is available in full-text in the database, all you need to do is print it out, e-mail it to your home, or save it to disk and you'll have the information that you need. If the article is for a periodical owned by the LRC but is not full-text in the database, use the information in the *Note* to locate the article in the Periodicals Room, in the

Reference Room with the bound volumes or in the microfilm cabinet. After you have located an appropriate article from microfilm you can print a copy; if found in a back issue you can make a photocopy.

Be aware that not all periodicals have the same level of authority, research, accuracy, or depth. When doing technical research, professional journals and trade journals will probably be the most useful. When doing academic research, scholarly journals, news magazines and newspapers with national circulation will probably be the most useful.

■ Summary

- ■ Developing good research skills now can help you to find materials quickly and efficiently later.
- ■ Select appropriate resources from the World Wide Web, periodicals and books based on the depth and the currency of the information that you need.
- ■ Find books that best answer your research questions by using all of the information presented in the online catalog.
- ■ Use periodical indexes and summaries to find appropriate articles quickly.
- ■ Evaluate each source of information for its value to the type of research that you are doing. Use the depth of data presented, its currency and the credentials of the author to judge the value of the information in resource materials.

Additional Resources

Resources in the Learning Resources Center (call numbers are shown in parentheses after the citation):

Basch, E. (1998). *Researching online for dummies.* Foster City, CA: IDG Books Worldwide. (TK5105.875 .I57 B374 1998)

Butler, J. A. (1998). *CyberSearch: Research techniques in the electronic age.* New York: Penguin. (ZA3075 .B88 1998)

Kennedy, S. D. (1998). *Best bet Internet: reference and research when you don't have time to mess around.* Chicago, IL: American Library Association. (ZA4201 .K46 1998)

Paul, N. & Williams, M. (1999). *Great scouts!: cyberguides for subject searching on the web.* Medford, NJ: Cyber Age Books. (ZA4201 .P38 1999)

Quarantiello, A. R. (2000). *The College student's research companion.* (2nd ed.). New York: Neal-Schuman Publishers. (Z710 .Q37 2000)

Woodward, J. A. (1997). *Writing research papers: investigating resources in cyberspace.* Lincolnwood, IL: NTC Publishing Group. (LB2369 .W66 1997)

Web Sites:

Please note that web site addresses often change. If you are unable to reach the addresses below, use a search engine and search the source of the site or the title of the web document to find the new site.

EBSCOhost: http://search.epnet.com

Library Catalogs
HELIN (Higher Education Library Information Network) Library Catalog: http://library.uri.edu/screens/opacmenu.html
Cooperating Libraries Automated Network: http://www.clan.lib.ri.us/
Library of Congress Online Catalog: http://catalog.loc.gov/

Virtual Libraries/Reference
Internet Public Library: http://www.ipl.org/ref/
Emory University's Virtual Library Project:
    http://www.library.emory.edu/VL/vlhome.html
refdesk.com: http://www.refdesk.com/
Best Information on the Net: http://vweb.sau.edu/bestinfo/

On-Campus Resources:

Learning Resources Center, Corner of Post Road and Baywood Street,
    (401) 739-5000, Ext. 3409.

Activity

8-1   Use the online catalog, EBSCOhost (online periodicals), or the Internet to find
      information that can help you answer your five career exploration questions.

CHAPTER 9
Developing Leadership Skills
Through Community Enrichment

"My motto is: Ask yourself what you want to do and go for it! I wanted to work in the automotive field and I wanted a degree. My experience at New England Tech has been wonderful. I came here because of the hands-on training; it really prepared me for my automotive technician position at New England Tire. I finished NEIT knowing that I am worth something, and I can be anything and be the best."

Luciano Nova
Automotive Technology

Chapter Designers:

Karen Arnold, Assistant Dean
Colette Recupero, Coordinator of Academic Services, Office of Teaching and Learning

What Students Are Saying . . .

"This is the most wonderful thing that I ever have done in my whole life. I always felt that helping other people by volunteering in the community brings experience and peace for the community. I also have more confidence which led me to believe in myself and ultimately the pursuit of my education. The greatest thing I have learned from this is the experience that led me to learn new responsibility for future leadership, communications, and compassion that will stay with me for the rest of my life."

Peter K. Thao
Electronics Technology, Class of 2000

In This Chapter

You will learn

- The requirements for the Community Enrichment Program.
- About your civic and social responsibilities.
- How to develop leadership skills through active volunteerism.
- About personal values and individual diversity.

■ Introduction

Developing Leadership Skills Through Community Enrichment introduces first quarter students to the requisite course TEC 102: Community Enrichment. Developed through New England Institute of Technology's Feinstein Enriching America Program, the Community Enrichment course is integrated into the core curriculum and complements the mission and values of the College. Community Enrichment encourages and supports all associate level students through an exploration of personal values, needs, strengths, skills, and civic responsibility in pursuit of a personally meaningful engagement with their communities. The course encompasses one class session; however, students may use the duration of their associate degree education to complete the community-based project or activity.

■ The Community Enrichment Experience

TEC 102: Community Enrichment, a Feinstein Enriching America Program, is a one-credit course required for graduation with an associate degree. The course involves three components:

1. The introductory class session;

2. Performance of a community-based project or activity, during which each student will become meaningfully involved in some facet of their community; and

3. Submission of a brief journal highlighting the community experience.

Enrichment vs. Service

The term "community enrichment" is distinguished from "community service" in terms of the student's approach to community involvement. The concept of "community service" often has negative or undesirable connotations associated with it, especially when the service is mandatory. Not only does our penal system use the term "community service" in awarding punishment for crimes committed, but the term "service" in and of itself may imply the giving of yourself as an obligation of servitude with no implicit benefit for the individual student. It is often considered work that is not necessarily personally meaningful and not the result of the student's informed choice regarding the type and extent of the service performed.

> **T**he Community Enrichment Experience should be good for the community—and for you.

Community Enrichment, on the other hand, implies that there is an inherent give and take for you and the community alike. You are provided an opportunity to utilize your individual and unique skills and interests for the benefit of the community, so you, as well as community members, gain from this experience. The Community Enrichment approach encourages you to choose thoughtfully how you best could become meaningfully engaged in a community-based activity. This approach recognizes each student as a unique individual in terms of strengths, interests, skills, needs, values and schedules. Therefore, each student brings a different set of expectations and benefits to their communities, which tend to be enriching for all involved.

Mission of the College

Developing Leadership Skills through Community Enrichment complements the mission of New England Institute of Technology. A paramount objective of NEIT is to "provide a campus climate where students are encouraged to respect the value of all people and to deal with the social problems and responsibilities they face as members of society" (NEIT Mission Statement #8). Thus, our students are provided the opportunity to use their individual skills, interests and technologies for the good of the community. We live and work in a democratic society; the term "democracy" meaning "a social condition of equality and respect for the individual within the community" (The American Heritage Dictionary, Houghton Mifflin, 1980).

Grading

You will receive an "IPR" grade, indicating "in progress" until you complete the requirements of the program. Upon completion of the requirements, you will receive a "P" grade, indicating "pass" and an additional credit will be awarded. The course must be completed by graduation with an associate's degree. Any student entering the bachelor's program needs to complete Community Enrichment prior to being admitted into that program.

Introductory Class Session

The classroom-based session for Community Enrichment is taken by all first quarter students through the TEC 101/102 curriculum. TEC 101 refers to this course, completed during the first quarter. TEC 102 refers to the Community Enrichment module only and may be completed over an eighteen month period of time (by week 10 of the sixth quarter).

Community-Based Volunteerism

All students will be responsible for choosing their own community project, activity or event to be performed during their associate's level education at NEIT. You are encouraged to identify your own individual strengths, needs, skills, interests and schedules in determining what type of project or activity best suits your needs. Although you are encouraged to perform approximately 15 hours of volunteerism in your community, counting your hours of volunteerism often has counterproductive results and defeats the purpose of being involved. Therefore, 15 hours is an approximate amount of time to be involved, and by no means mandatory. Once you have chosen an activity that is personally meaningful *and* felt that involvement had a significant impact on the lives of others, you have fulfilled your obligation to the community. As a result of the individualized approach to community-based activities, NEIT's students tend to contribute an average of 60–80 hours in projects addressing community needs.

> **Y** ou can have a significant impact on the lives of others by sharing your time and your skills.

Guidelines for Choosing Community Projects/ Activities/Events

Keeping the following guidelines in mind, students may choose *any* community-based activity.

1. The activity should be **personally meaningful**. Explore your values, interests and technology and choose a project that complements who you are as a person.

2. The activity should be with a **non-profit** organization, *or* for an individual(s) representing a community **"need."** Individuals representing a "need" of the community include people who are not physically, financially, or mentally able to perform certain tasks, responsibilities or daily living skills without the assistance of others. This category includes, but is not limited to, individuals who are elderly, physically or mentally disabled, terminally ill and those on a fixed income who cannot afford to hire professionals for basic and necessary repairs and tasks.

3. The work performed is **voluntary**. It is not appropriate for you to receive financial rewards or commodities in exchange for community-based volunteer activities.

4. The project/activity/event should address an actual **community need** and should have a significant impact on the lives of others. Engaging in work with a non-profit organization will definitely address a need of the community, the most global of which is helping the organization to fulfill its mission or purpose. If you choose to help *individuals*, however, you should guarantee the "need of the community" by asking yourself, "Does this individual have the physical or financial resources to either perform the task himself or to hire/pay someone to do it?" If the answer is yes, then it does not represent a genuine need of the community. Another caution with assisting individuals is the potential confusion between addressing a "community need" versus "social/familial obligations." You should carefully consider the needs of individuals when performing tasks for community members and not confuse this work with a social or family obligation.

Four Guidelines for Community Projects

■ *personally meaningful*

■ *for a non-profit organization*

■ *voluntary*

■ *address a community need*

Writing the Community Enrichment Journal

The journal is a simple three-paragraph essay written at the culmination of the project to highlight your community-based experience. Please adhere to the following guidelines while writing your journal:

1. **Facts** of the project/activity/event
   - Describe the organization and its role in the community.
   - Describe your functions or role within this activity.
   - How many hours did you volunteer? Between what dates?

2. **How did YOU benefit** from this experience?
   - What did you gain?
   - What did you learn (about yourself, the community, others) from this experience?

3. **How did OTHERS benefit** from your involvement?
   - Describe your **impact** on the community, organization, or individual.

For completion of the requirements of TEC 102: Community Enrichment, students must submit the journal along with the project documentation form to the Feinstein Enriching America Office.

■ Social Responsibility

It is the responsibility of every person, regardless of race, age, income or citizenship to address some issue of concern afflicting our communities. The very nature of living, working, gaining an education and interacting with other individuals in our society makes everyone susceptible to the civic responsibilities inherent in each of our communities. A "community" entails much more than just the geographical environs of a particular area. "Community" refers to the people living and working within a geographical zone and the social interactions between them. Hence, a community is comprised of the people who work and are educated in a neighborhood, share similar resources and engage meaningfully with one another.

In any given community, there is a vast array of social issues and concerns challenging the people and/or environment. Issues such as polluted waterways, ineffective educational systems, teenage pregnancy, substance abuse and domestic violence are only a few such concerns. Although each community has a different set of social problems, many of these issues encompass a broader scope than others and have far reaching detrimental effects on an entire population. Due to the scope of social and environmental problems plaguing our society, it is the responsibility of every person to make this world a better place in which to live. These issues afflicting our communities are not going to resolve themselves if community members do not become actively involved in addressing these concerns. Since each person is a unique individual with differing values and interests, contributing to the solution of different social problems will appeal to different people. Thus, it is your responsibility to explore your own unique values and interests and determine how these unique characteristics would best address a need of the community.

It may be helpful for you to consider the following in determining your own personal venue for civic responsibility:

- Take time to learn about groups, ideas and causes that interest you.
- What social or neighborhood problems concern you?
- Does volunteering for one of these groups fit your own interest?
- How much time do you have to commit?
- What activities do you enjoy doing? How do you have fun?
- What talents or skills do you have to offer?
- What do you want to get out of your involvement?

Developing Leadership Skills Through Active Volunteerism

"I feel that when we perform acts of kindness, not just others, but we ourselves, benefit; we develop a sense of camaraderie and leadership, as well as social skills unavailable in any textbook. In order for us to provide for ourselves, we must provide for others. It is vital to the progression of society for people to work together in an attempt to make our world a better place to live."

Jonathon Bunker
Architectural/Building Engineering Technology, Class of 1998

Community involvement fosters leadership as well as many other valuable and marketable skills. As an active volunteer seeking social justice, a cleaner environment, better educational systems, access for individuals with disabilities or other similar concerns, students are immersed in various aspects of democracy, seeking equal rights and respect for all individuals. Volunteerism helps you develop capacities for self-actualization, self-esteem, pride and teamwork—all qualities which foster leadership skills. Successful community-based programs indicate that you have the potential to gain the following benefits from being involved:

- increased self-esteem
- increased confidence
- new skills
- sense of accomplishment or pride
- career awareness
- learning by doing: active and effective learning
- leadership skills
- racial and ethnic tolerance
- interpersonal and communication skills
- social responsibility

Personal Values and Individual Diversity

Values are personal qualities that lead to moral excellence. It is important for you to thoughtfully explore your own individual set of values prior to embarking upon a community-based project in order to maximize the personal meaning of the chosen activity. As mentioned earlier, each individual possesses a unique set of values, interests and needs. Often, values are a result of your culture, upbringing, education and personal experiences. Given the individual diversity that comprises our society, no two people have the same set of values or needs. What values are important or desirable to **you**?

Listed below are several values to consider. Please remember that this list is by no means exhaustive and you are encouraged to note additional personal qualities.

Caring	Compassion	Sincerity
Responsibility	Respect for Others	Respect for Self
Honesty	Dependability	Education
Familiarity	Clean Environment	Social Justice/Equality
Listening	Civic Involvement	Integrity
Spirituality/Religion	Compatibility	Versatility
Sense of Humor	Generosity	Friendships/family
Happiness	Empathy	Independence
Interpersonal Skills	Positive Role Model	Understanding
Communication	Patience	Tolerance
Trust		

■ Summary

- TEC 102: Community Enrichment may be completed over the duration of your associate degree education; it must be completed prior to graduation
- Community Enrichment has 3 components:
  - In-class introductory session
  - Performance of a community-based project/activity/event
  - Submission of a journal highlighting the community experience
- Community-based projects should be:
  - Personally meaningful
  - For a non-profit organization or individual representing a need
  - Volunteer
  - Meeting an actual community need
- Essays highlighting the student's community involvement should address:
  - The FACTS
  - How you personally benefitted from this experience
  - What impact your involvement had on the community or others

Additional Resources

Resources in the Learning Resources Center (call numbers are shown in parentheses after the citation):

Blank, R. & Slipp, S. (1994). *Voices of diversity: real people talk about problems and solutions in a workplace where everyone is not alike.* New York: Amacom. (HF5549.5 .M5 B55 1994)

Kretzmann, J. P. & McKnight, J. L. (1993). *Building communities from the inside out: a path toward finding and mobilizing a community's assets.* Evanston, IL: Center for Urban Affairs and Policy Research, Neighborhood Innovations Network, Northwestern University. (HN90 .C6 K748 1993)

McGuckin, F. (Ed.). (1998). *Volunteerism.* New York: H.W. Wilson Co. (HN79 .V63 V65 1998)

Web Sites:

Please note that web site addresses often change. If you are unable to reach the addresses below, use a search engine and search the source of the site or the title of the web document to find the new site.

Alternative Break Program—Break Away:
    http://www.alternativebreaks.com
America's Promise—Volunteer Summit Information:
    http://www.Americaspromise.org
America Reads: http://www.cns.gov/areads/
Campus Outreach Opportunity League (COOL): http://www.cool2serve.org
Community College Service-Learning Resources:
    http://www.aacc.nche.edu/initiatives/projects.htm
Corporation for National Service: http://www.cns.gov
Feinstein Enriching America Program:
    http://www.feinsteinfoundation.com/college.html
National Service-Learning Cooperative Clearinghouse:
    http://www.nicsl.coled.umn.edu/
National Service Resource Center: http://www.etr.org/NSRC
On-Campus Service-Learning (OCSL): http://www.umich.edu/~mserve/
R.I. Campus Compact:
    http://www.brown.edu/Departments/Swearer_Center/RICC/
Service Site—finding volunteer opportunities in your community:
    http://www.servenet.org
Service-Learning Home Page: http://www.nicsl.coled.umn.edu/
SCALE—National Literacy Program: http://www.unc.edu/depts/scale

On-Campus Resources:

Feinstein Enriching America Program Office, Center for the Technologies, Second
    Floor, (401) 739-5000, Ext. 3322.

Activity

Submit a written narrative (journal) upon completion of your community experience. *Note:* You have the duration of your Associate Degree program to submit the written narrative.

9-1   Fill out the Timeline for Completion of Community Project sheet.

9-2   To receive full credit for the completion of TEC 102, you must submit the Documentation of Performance of Community Project form (Appendix, p. 170).

- AND -

9-3   Submit a brief journal highlighting your community-based experience (Appendix, p. 171). *Note:* You have the duration of your associate degree program to submit the written narrative.

■ Activity 9-1. Timeline for Completion of Community Project

Student Name: _____ Date: _____

TEC 101/102 Section #: _____

1. What values / interests / skills do you possess that could benefit the community?

2. Develop a brief timeline for your completion of the Community Enrichment requisite:

CHAPTER 10
Looking Ahead:
Career and Beyond

"I was determined to find a career to support my son and myself so I enrolled in the Manufacturing Engineering Technology program. I found it a challenge in that I had no prior knowledge of manufacturing and was the only female in my class; however, I received a great deal of support from the faculty. They gave me confidence that I could succeed. After finishing my AS degree, I continued on for my bachelor's degree. I am now in engineering at Polyflex. NEIT has helped me gain more than I could have dreamed: I have gained my life and a wonderful future with my son."

Nancy Ferrera
Manufacturing Engineering Technology

Chapter Designers:

Sharon J. Charette, Learning Resources Center Director
Stephanie Ferriola, Competency-Based Faculty Development
Catherine Kennedy, Vice President for Career Development

What Students Are Saying . . .

"I was approaching my 30th birthday and had begun to realize that I had reached the top of the proverbial "glass ceiling" as far as my career was concerned. I knew that without an advanced education, I would not be able to proceed any higher so I enrolled at NEIT . . . My experience here can be summarized in one word, rewarding. This college reinforced my belief that if I put my heart and soul into the curriculum, I could succeed. I learned that the harder I work, the better the reward and that I control my own destiny. I am working at EMC Corporation and earning a much higher salary than what I earned before returning to school."

Gerard Lebrun
Computer Information Systems Technology

In This Chapter

You will learn how to

- Conduct an informational interview to get a clear picture of the requirements of your chosen occupation.
- Package your career portfolio and create a resume that leaves a good first impression with a prospective employer.

■ Introduction

As a new student, you have already completed the process of making a career choice. By learning as much as possible about your new field you can concentrate on acquiring the skills and experience that will make you marketable to employers.

You can never begin too soon to collect the information you will need for a resume and the elements that make up a career portfolio. By thinking about what you need at the beginning of your college career and collecting what you need while in school, you will be armed with a thoughtfully prepared resume and portfolio when you graduate and begin your job search.

■ Reading: Internship and Career Preparation

"How do I use my college experience to prepare for an internship or career?" you might wonder. Well, before you visit any advisor or seek out any further help, the first step is to relax. Take a deep breath and keep in mind that your experiences should be viewed as stepping stones for a future internship or career.

In this chapter, we will present to you some ways in which you can begin to plan for a career. We will supply you with the resources necessary for you to find the career or internship which is just right for you. Of course, there is not one road which is right for everyone. Thus, you need to take a look at the model which we have supplied for you and realize what will work best for you. As an individual, you must realize where your knowledge, skills, and desire lie. Only then will you be able to find the career or internship which suits you best.

Career Planning Model

Supplied here is a career planning model. Please keep in mind that this is just one model to plan your career. Planning your career is an on-going process and the steps supplied here only provide a framework for you to find out what will fit best with your life.

I. Step one is self-awareness. By developing a clear understanding of yourself, your values, your interests, your abilities, and your aspirations, you can begin to uncover what it is that you want out of a career and out of an internship. An understanding of self is facilitated by taking exploratory classes and consulting career counselors. Additionally, you can attend workshops, get involved with activities and clubs, and communicate feelings and ideas with others.

II. Step two is career exploration. By utilizing your self-awareness, you can begin to consider the most interesting and/or logical career and major for you. Explore by researching employment opportunities and job descriptions. Remember to choose a related major according to your possible career interests. By always investigating and exploring alternatives, you will be sure to leave no door closed and no stone unturned.

III. Step three is preparation for career. Continue to narrow your job search by enhancing skills and gaining knowledge and experience. You can achieve such by taking part in internships, seeking related summer employment, and volunteering. Additionally, you can take part in campus activities, do related research, and take courses applicable to your intended career. Developing a rapport with faculty is also beneficial.

IV. Step four, the ultimate goal, is to start working. After becoming more aware of yourself, exploring different careers, and preparing for the career of your choice, you are almost ready to start working. Now is the time to put the finishing touches on the career of your choice. The perfect career can be found by preparing your resume and practicing for interviews. Remember to trust the validity of your experience. By utilizing all contacts, attending job fairs, and contacting employment agencies, you can explore all of the possible employment opportunities available to you.

Career Preparation

Now, let us take the time to focus more on the career preparation aspect of our career planning model. The vital aspect of career preparation provides important experience which cannot be gained from the classroom. Networking is vital to your career preparation. Networking is created by the contacts and relationships that are built through the experiences which help you to prepare for your career. These contacts and relationships can prove to be of great benefit in gaining entrance to your career choice. They can also help you build your resume.

Remember that there are numerous resources and opportunities available to assist you as you search for the perfect internship or career. Utilize the resources which are available. Also, the internet can provide you access to an endless number of job lists and other employment opportunities.

Good Luck! And remember, to find the perfect internship and career for you, you must explore every opportunity and resource available to you.

◼ Reading: Informational Interviewing

Informational interviewing is an intentional strategy which provides you with a direct means of collecting information on your prospective career from individuals who are currently employed in your field. Informational interviewing is one of the most effective forms of networking.

It is a means of connecting with others to form relationships which have immediate and future employment potential. You can obtain a job through networking.

Important: Remember that you are not asking for a job. You are simply collecting information in order to better understand the realities of a particular occupation.

You should try to secure two more names of people you could meet from the person you are interviewing. Also, remember to *always* follow up with a thank you letter.

What to Find Out Through an Informational Interview

Consider these questions:

- ◼ What do you like/dislike about your job?
- ◼ What college courses/experiences were most helpful for you?
- ◼ Is certification or an advanced degree necessary for the job?
- ◼ Are there any professional groups you would recommend I join?
- ◼ What was your career path?
- ◼ Which part of the job is most challenging for you?
- ◼ What are the qualifications you look for in hiring entry-level employees?
- ◼ What experiences have you had that you think have been invaluable to your learning this field?
- ◼ If you could do it all over again, would you choose the same path for yourself? What would you have done differently?
- ◼ What do you see as future trends in this industry?
- ◼ What are the job titles of the positions I would most likely be applying for?
- ◼ What can I do to make myself a better candidate?
- ◼ Could you suggest someone else in the field whom I may contact?

(from Zaugra, J. (1998). *The Student Career Portfolio: a helpful guide for career assessment, goal planning, documentation and utilization.* Madison, WI: Mendota Press.)

◼ Creating a Portfolio

In addition to a resume and cover letter, a portfolio is a good way to highlight your talents and accomplishments for a potential employer. Since the items displayed in a portfolio represent a life's work, you can begin collecting samples at the beginning of your college career—well in advance of applying for a position.

What to Include in a Portfolio

The following list includes suggestions for items that are typically included in a portfolio. You may come up with additional items based on your work experience, educational background, and special talents.

- Resume.
- List of portfolio contents.
- List of special skills if not included in your resume.
- Copy of diplomas, transcripts, certificates of completion for courses or special training, or any documents that verify certification. Only include transcripts if your grade point average is 3.0 or above. All of these items provide documentation of your educational and training accomplishments.
- Samples of work that you have done. This may include writing samples, designs, drawings, publications, photographs, and, in some cases, audio cassettes or videotapes. A program from an event that you took part in might also be included.
- List of conferences or workshops attended that relate to your skills or career goals.
- Awards and recommendations. Include recommendations, thank you letters from colleagues, customers or supervisors, performance reviews from work as well as honors and awards received.
- Memberships. List any memberships that indicate a commitment to the community, your chosen profession or to any other valuable pursuit. This part of the portfolio will show that you are a well-rounded individual. Do not list any controversial, religious or political memberships that could unfavorably influence a potential employer.
- Other. Any other information related to your achievements and talents. This might include information about your Feinstein Community Enrichment project, newspaper articles or any other samples or documents that illustrate your value to an employer.

You can begin to collect the items for your portfolio right away. It is best to begin assembling parts of your portfolio at the time when awards are achieved, degrees are earned and honors are bestowed. This will save you many hours trying to hunt down the elements of your portfolio right before your interview. Remember—the portfolio is one of the most important tools that you can use to sell your accomplishments to an employer. It should be updated regularly as new events occur in your life.

Reading: Packaging Your Portfolio

What Your Portfolio Might Look Like

All portfolios are unique and represent particular traits, goals, and experiences of individuals. Portfolios reflect notable personal attributes and their development over a period of time during your undergraduate years. Portfolios reflect samples of work and achievement.

Your portfolio describes and defines your distinctiveness. It should not be like other portfolios. It is your uniqueness which emerges through the development and documentation of your traits. Develop it to distinguish yourself from others.

Here are some ideas which you might consider to use when putting your portfolio together. General content guidelines include:

1. Cover Page. Design your own cover page. Consider using a variety of ink or page colors, various font sizes, and/or visual aids.

(from Zaugra, J. (1998). *The Student Career Portfolio: a helpful guide for career assessment, goal planning, documentation and utilization*. Madison, WI: Mendota Press.)

2. Table of Contents. Arrange your portfolio according to career and personal themes. Use themes, like career assessment and development, goal planning, working with mentors, internship, samples of work, volunteerism, awards and certificates, special training and/or degrees and references. Each section of the portfolio is different from others.

3. Labels. For each section of the portfolio, use a different title or label. Consider color coding the labels.

4. Sheet Protectors. Use "nonstick" polypropylene sheets. Such sheets won't remove ink from printed pages. Use medium weight sheets and top loading sheets for easy access to portfolio items for updates and to prevent the records of your accomplishments from being lost or misplaced.

5. Notebook or Binder. Consider placing your sheets in a binder arranged according to the sections of your portfolio.

6. Notebook or Binder Size. If you maintained a record of all achievements, your notebook portfolio can be become large. Remember, during an interview—only use those samples of your work germane to the career/job interview.

■ Reading: Using Your Portfolio

(Adapted from Zaugra, J. (1998). *The Student Career Portfolio: a helpful guide for career assessment, goal planning, documentation and utilization*. Madison, WI: Mendota Press.)

As you complete your academic work at New England Tech, use your portfolio to:

1. Further develop your interests, skills and abilities;

2. Work with your academic advisor, career mentor and college instructors; and

3. Record your growth, development and achievements.

Your portfolio documentation will be useful to you in the workplace as well. Use it to

1. Present yourself in the job interview. Remember: the portfolio should support the interview conversation, not drive it. To learn more about how to present your portfolio, consider the interviewing Assistance available through the Career Services Office;

2. Demonstrate how you developed yourself as a student at New England Tech; and

3. Seek job promotions and advancements.

■ Preparing a Resume

A resume serves as a snapshot of you and what you have to offer an employer. Most employers will spend approximately 30 seconds screening resumes. At a later time, they will read in more detail the resumes that caught their interest. When you apply for a job, the resume must speak for you by carefully summarizing your experience, education and background. It is important to supply truthful, correct information. Potential employers often check with your previous employer to

A resume speaks for you—be sure it says the right things.

verify that the information you have included is accurate. Stretching the truth too much—or worse yet, lying—could cost you the position for which you are applying.

Content and Appearance

1. The resume of recent graduates is usually no more than one page long. (It should fill one complete page.) Some grads may need a two page resume if appropriate for their prior work history. Two common styles of resumes are a chronological resume, which lists employment history in reverse chronological order and a functional resume, which emphasizes skills. Examples of both types of resumes are included later in this chapter.

2. The appearance of your resume is very important and should be appealing to the reader. Use space wisely by arranging your information to fit on one page. Your resume should be printed on heavy stock paper using a laser printer. You have your choice of color; however, it is best to stay with a conservative color such as white, ivory, or gray. For a professional resume package, the same paper should be used for your cover letter and envelope.

3. **Spelling should be absolutely perfect.** Spelling and typing errors will most likely remove you from consideration. Pronouns are usually not used on resumes. Information should be presented in a concise manner using key words and descriptive phrases.

4. As your work experience changes, so should your resume. It is very important to always have an updated resume. Handwritten additions or changes to your resume are inappropriate.

5. Resumes have several sections that will vary for each person. Important information that qualifies you for the position for which you are applying should be placed toward the top of your resume.

Most Commonly Used Sections

Contact Information: Your **name**, **current address** and a **telephone number** where you can be reached should always be the most prominent piece of information at the top of the page. If you have a FAX number or an E-mail address, it would be appropriate to place those after your telephone number.

Objective: Optional. An objective is used to state your career goals. If you have more than one goal, you may need more than one resume. Many recent grads include this section to help fill a one page resume.

Education: For recent grads this section usually holds the most value. Be sure to completely write out your degree and technology. You may include the skills acquired in your technology under education or in a separate skills section. NEIT's Career Services Office recommends that a GPA of 3.0 or higher be included on the resume of recent grads.

Skills or Summary of Qualifications: This section may appear before or after the education section. You should include skills which enhance your marketability, regardless of where they were acquired (school, employment, self-taught, volunteer experience, etc.). Computer skills should always be listed regardless of your technology. You should use *key words* related to your field; this would include all technical terms. Many employers will screen resumes by using key words when considering which candidates to interview.

Related Experience: Internships or jobs that are related to the career or position for which you are applying should be listed in this section. Be sure to state that it was an internship when listing it as related experience.

Employment: Usually resumes include your last three to four jobs or past ten years of employment (if you have held only one or two positions during this period). List the name of the company, city, state, your job title, dates of employment, and a **brief** description of your job duties and responsibilities. Be sure to tailor this section to those duties that would best relate to the position for which you are applying. Whenever possible, include accomplishments with measurable results.

Memberships: Membership in organizations affiliated with your field/technology should be included. Do not list any controversial memberships (such as religious or political organizations).

Awards and Accomplishments: Optional. This section should highlight any awards or achievements earned that would round out your professional and/or personal character. Awards earned in college or within the community are appropriate.

Interests/Hobbies: Optional. Be careful with this section and do not list any controversial hobbies or interests (subjects such as religion, politics, etc.). List interests that show you are a well-rounded person. A mixture of cultural, physical, and leisure interests will be more impressive than several interests of the same type.

Personal: Optional. Never put your age, marital status or number of children on your resume. List personal skills that may be pertinent to the position for which you are applying. If you are bilingual, it is important to include any languages that you speak or write fluently.

References: Optional. If you choose to include this section, it should be stated that References Are Available Upon Request. If you are in a technology in which it is appropriate to have a reel or portfolio, it should be stated that References and Reel, or References and Portfolio Are Available Upon Request. The References themselves should be typed on a separate sheet of paper and centered from top to bottom on the page. References are normally from employers and supervisors or from college instructors. Usually three to five names are listed along with their job titles, full addresses and telephone numbers. Always ask permission *before* listing someone as a reference. This will give your references a chance to prepare should they be asked to speak about your qualifications for a position.

John H. Smith

29 Greenwood Street
Warwick, Rhode Island 02886
(401) 555-1234

OBJECTIVE: A position in the HVAC field offering a challenge and opportunity for growth.

EDUCATION: **New England Institute of Technology**
Warwick, Rhode Island
Associate in Science Degree, March 2000
Refrigeration, Air Conditioning, Heating and Gas Technology
G.P.A. 3.65

<u>**A hands-on program which included:**</u>
Mechanical and electrical control devices
Installation and troubleshooting HVAC systems
Service call procedures
Basic electricity
Servicing gas-fired furnaces, boilers, water heaters, and rooftop systems

EPA Refrigerant Transition and Recovery Certification, Type I

EMPLOYMENT: **Auto Express Center,** Providence, Rhode Island
Assistant Manager
Supervise eight employees and ensure excellent customer service. Solely
responsible for all administrative functions.
<u>Accomplishment</u>: Increased store profits by 30% in a two-year period.
1998 - Present

Eddie's Service Station, Warwick, Rhode Island
Technician
Performed oil changes, lubes and preventive maintenance on motor vehicles.
Acquired excellent mechanical skills.
1993 - 1998

Food Land Supermarket, Providence, Rhode Island
Head Clerk
Supervised stock clerks and handled customer complaints. Assisted in product
display and inventory.
1991 - 1993

COMMUNITY
SERVICE: **Warwick Elementary School,** Warwick, Rhode Island
America Reads Program - Assist with First and Second Grade reading classes.
1999 - Present

Sample chronological resume

Alex J. Bouchard

21 Bell Avenue • Coventry, Rhode Island 02882
(401) 555-1234 • Email: Alexb@ids.com

EDUCATION: **New England Institute of Technology, Warwick, Rhode Island**
Bachelor's Degree in Electronics Engineering Technology, 2000
GPA 3.65

Associate Degree in Electronics Technology, 1998
GPA 3.88

**ELECTRONIC
BACKGROUND:** Industrial Motor Controls, Robotics, Circuit Analysis, Microcontrollers and
Data Communications.

Skills: Building and troubleshooting AC/DC, analog and digital circuits. Test
equipment (oscilloscope, function generator, frequency counter and digital
multimeter).

Senior Design Project: The design and building of a working 4 bit computer
on B^2 Logic (Digital Simulation Software) for Digital Lab Development.
Results: A working 4 bit computer with step-by-step detailed technical manual
finished 2 weeks before deadline.

**COMPUTER
SKILLS:**
Languages:
Motorola 68000/Intel 8031 Assembly, Machine, Quick C and Quick Basic
Software:
Novell Netware 3.12, Orcad, MS Works, MS Word, MS Excel, MS Windows
and B^2 Logic. Programmable Logic Controllers (Modsoft, Allen Bradley and
Paragon)

EMPLOYMENT: **New England Institute of Technology,** Warwick, RI   (Present/part-time)
Instructor Assistant, Lab Assistant and Theory Tutor for Electronics
Technology

Ribco Electronics, Cranston, RI   (Present/part-time)
PC technician installing boards and wiring for Novell networks

Coventry Wholesalers Club, Coventry, RI   (1981 - 1997)
Office Manager, Computerized employee, inventory and financial records
Results: 50% cost savings in record keeping

ACTIVITIES: Hiking, Bicycling, Traveling, and Community Outreach Center Volunteer

Sample chronological resume

CHRISTINE MASON

115 Heroux Boulevard
Cumberland, Rhode Island 02864
(401) 555-1234
Email: Cmason@aol.com

OBJECTIVE

A position as an electronics technician with a preference for field service.

EDUCATION

New England Institute of Technology, Warwick, Rhode Island
Associate in Science Degree in Electronics Technology, December 1999
G.P.A. 3.98

SUMMARY OF SKILLS

Electronics
Skilled in the construction and troubleshooting of electronic circuits, AC and DC theory and applications, basic and advanced analog devices, digital devices and microprocessors. Fiber optic technology including hands-on use of OTDR, splicing and terminating. Soldered and tuned a discrete AM/FM radio.

Computer
Windows 3.X, Windows 95 & 97, Microsoft Office 97, Works, and WordPerfect.

Mechanical
Small repairs on cars and other motors, very mechanically inclined.

Construction
Roofing, painting, sheetrock, repair work, and remodeling. Ability to work with a variety of tools.

EMPLOYMENT

Wal-Mart, North Attleboro, Massachusetts
POS ordering and inventory on computer and hand held terminal, stocking, set-up displays for visual appeal, ensure excellent customer service.
1992 - Present

REFERENCES

Available upon request

Sample functional/combination resume

■ Cover Letters

A cover letter serves as an introduction to your resume. Therefore, a cover letter should always be included when you mail a resume to an employer. When you meet with an employer in person, you do not need a cover letter.

Your cover letter and resume should be sent to the person in a position to do the hiring. His/her name should be included in the inside address at the top of the cover letter.

The body of the letter has three parts and should be written in three to four paragraphs.

Part One: Why are you submitting your resume? If applicable, mention where you saw the ad. If you were referred by someone, mention the name of the person. If you are submitting the cover letter and resume with no knowledge of an opening, include the name of the position (or department) for which you are applying.

Part Two: Why should the employer consider you for an interview? Include information about your skills, training and work experience that qualifies you for the position for which you are applying. Whenever possible, mention something you know about the company.

Part Three: Express your interest in an interview and how you can be reached. (It is important to have an answering machine or voice mail for your phone messages.)

(Down 5 - 6 lines)

123 Medway Street
Providence, RI 02906
March 30, 2000

(Down 3 - 5 lines)

Mr. William Bell
Director of MIS
Hi-Tec Company
1920 Smith Street
Providence, RI 02906
(Down 2 lines)

Dear Mr. Bell:
(Down 2 lines)

Please accept the enclosed resume as application for the position of network administrator assistant. I am confident that my educational background and strong interest in the computer field will enable me to make a significant contribution to your facility.

I received hands-on training in computer servicing and networking through my education at New England Tech. I understand that Hi-Tec's MIS department supports a Novell network and was recently highlighted in this month's issue of the *Providence Business News*. I am skilled in the service and support of Novell Netware, and the installation and configuration of Windows 3.x and 95. I am also a Certified Network Administrator (CNA).

In addition, I possess excellent mechanical and troubleshooting skills as well as a great work ethic. My performance evaluations have been consistently excellent, and I have often been commended for my willingness to work long, irregular hours.

I would like the opportunity to discuss the possibility of becoming a member of your MIS department. You can reach me at (401) 555-0000. I am looking forward to hearing from you.

(Down 2 - 3 lines)

Sincerely,
(Down 4 lines)

Nancy Riley

Nancy Riley

Sample cover letter

The appearance of your cover letter counts

■ *It should be only one page.*

■ *Use a printer that has letter quality typeface.*

■ *The cover letter should be printed on paper that matches your resume.*

■ *Sign your name in ink above your typed signature on the copy to be mailed.*

When mailing the cover letter, placing it on top of the resume and fold them both in thirds. They should be placed in a matching envelope. The address on the envelope should always be typed.

■ Summary

■ Internships are a useful means of learning about your new career and getting some job experience before you graduate from college.

■ Conducting an informational interview is a good way to collect information about your prospective career and to network with people in that field.

■ A portfolio supports the information in your resume by providing samples and documents that illustrate your accomplishments.

■ A carefully prepared resume is the most important tool for securing a job interview.

■ A cover letter serves as an introduction to your resume and highlights the experience that most qualifies you for the job that you seek.

Additional Resources

Resources in the Learning Resources Center (call numbers are shown in parentheses after the citation):

The Adams job interview almanac. (1996). Holbrook, MA: Adams Media Corp. (Career Planning HF5549.5 .I6 A3 1996)

Angel, D. L. & Harney, E. E. (1997). *No one is unemployable: creative solutions for overcoming barriers to employment.* Hacienda Heights, CA: WorkNet Publications. (Career Planning HF5381 .A7857 1997)

Battle, C. W. (1994). *Smart maneuvers: taking control of your career and personal success in the Information Age.* New York: Allworth Press. (HF5386 .B28 1994)

Beatty, R. H. (1998). *The five-minute interview.* (2nd Ed.). New York: Wiley. (Career Planning HF5549.5 .I6 B39 1998)

Cochran, C. & Peerce, D. (1999). *Heart and soul Internet job search: 7 never-before-published secrets to capturing your dream job using the Internet.* Palo Alto, CA: Davies-Black Publishing. (Career Planning HF 5382.7 .C6 1999)

Fry, R. W. (1996). *Your first interview.* Franklin Lakes, NJ: Career Press. (Career Planning HF5549.5 .I6 F76 1996)

Gonyea, J. C. & Gonyea, W. M. (1996). *Electronic resumes: a complete guide to putting your resume on-line.* New York: McGraw-Hill. (Career Planning HF5383 .G55 1996)

Gonyea, J. C. (1995). *The on-line job search companion: a complete guide to hundreds of career planning and job hunting resources available via your computer.* New York: McGraw-Hill. (Career Planning HF5382.75 .U6 G66 1995)

Hansen, K. (1998). *Dynamic cover letters for new graduates.* Berkeley, CA: Ten Speed Press. (Career Planning HF5383 .H278 1998)

Krannich, R. L. & Krannich, C. R. (1998). *The best jobs for the 21st century.* Manassas Park, VA: Impact Publications. (Career Planning HF5382 .K68 1998)

Weddle, P. D. (1995). *Electronic resumes for the new job market.* Manassas Park, VA: Impact Publications. (Career Planning HF5383 .W324 1995)

Weinstein, B. (1996). *So what if I'm 50?: straight talk and proven strategies for getting hired in the toughest job market ever.* New York: McGraw-Hill. (Career Planning HF5382.7 .W444 1996)

Zaugra, J. (1998). *The student career portfolio: a helpful guide for career assessment, goal planning, documentation and utilization.* Madison, WI: Mendota Press. (Career Planning HF5381 .Z38 1998)

Web Sites:

Please note that web site addresses often change. If you are unable to reach the addresses below, use a search engine and search the source of the site or the title of the web document to find the new site.

See the extensive list of career-related Web Sites in Chapter 6.

Professional Organizations
Accuracy in Media: http://www.aim.org
AFL-CIO: http://www.aflcio.org/
Air Conditioning & Refrigeration Institute: http://www.ari.org
American Accounting Association: http://accounting.rutgers.edu/raw/aaa/
American Association of Medical Assistants: http://www.AAMA-ntl.org
American Boatbuilders and Repairer's Association (ABBRA): http://www.abbra.org
American Boat & Yacht Council (ABYC): http://www.abycinc.org
American Institute of Certified Public Accountants:
     http://www.rutgers.edu/Accounting/raw/aicpa/home.htm
American Medical Technologists: http://www.AMT1.com
American Physical Therapy Association: http://www.apta.org
American Society for Training & Development:
     http://www.astd.org/virtual_community/find/
American Society of Mechanical Engineers: http://www.asme.org
American Gas Association: http://www.aga.org
American Society of Heating, Refrigeration & Air Conditioning Engineers:
     http://www.ashrae.org
American Society for Testing & Materials: http://www.cssinfo.com/info/astm.html
American Occupational Therapy Association: http://www.aota.org
Association of Surgical Technologists: http://www.ast.org
Better Business Bureau: http://www.bbb.org
Building Officials & Code Administrators International: http://www.bocai.org
Future Business Leaders of America: http://www.fbla-pbl.org/
Industrial Designers Society of America: http://www.idsa.org
Institute of Electrical and Electronics Engineers, Inc. (IEEE):
     http://www.ieee.org/
International Association of Administrative Professionals:
     http://www.goldencorridor.org
International Interior Design Association: http://www.iida.org
International Federation of Robotics: http://www.ifr.org
National Association of Oil Heating Service Managers: http://www.naohsm.org
National Association of Broadcasters: http://www.nab.org

National Health Information Center: http://nhic-nt.health.org
National Automobile Dealers Association: http://www.nada.org
National Marine Manufacturer's Association (NMMA): http://www.nmma.org
Natural Gas Information and Educational Resources: http://www.naturalgas.org
NetWare Users Group: http://www.novell.com/corp/community/nui/index.html
Plumbing-Heating-Cooling Contractors Association: http://www.naphcc.org
Small Business Rhode Island: http://www.sbaonline.sba.gov/regions/states/ri
Society of Manufacturing Engineers: http://www.sme.org
Society for Neuroscience: http://www.sfn.org
Society of Broadcast Engineers: http://www.sbe.org
Southern New England Network Users Group: http://www.snenug.org/
Windows Users Group Network: http://www.wugnet.com/

On-Campus Resources:

Office of Career Services, Center for the Technologies, Second Floor, (401) 739-5000, Ext. 3458.

Learning Resources Center, Corner of Post Road and Baywood Street, (401) 739-5000, Ext. 3409.

APPENDIX

![Career Inventory Folder icon] Career Inventory Folder

The Career Inventory Folder will be an ongoing part of your career planning process. As an ongoing process, this folder and its contents should be kept as documentation of your progress in achieving academic and career goals. Before you graduate, you should have a portfolio ready to bring to a prospective employer that will show evidence of your employability.

In fulfillment of TEC 101 requirements, the Career Inventory Folder must include the following assignments:

Module/ Chapter	Assignment	Number of Points	Completed?
2	Completed Goal Setting Worksheet	10	
5	Computer Skills Assessment Chart	10	
2 through 9	Five Career Exploration Questions and Answers	20	
Appendix	Self-Assessment/Reflective Memo	20	
	Total Number of Points	60	

■ Activity 2-1. Goal-Setting Worksheet

_____-Term Goal:

Action Plan

Action/Strategy (Be Specific)	How	Time Invested	When Completed

Activity 2-1. Goal-Setting Worksheet

TIME LINE TOWARD GRADUATION

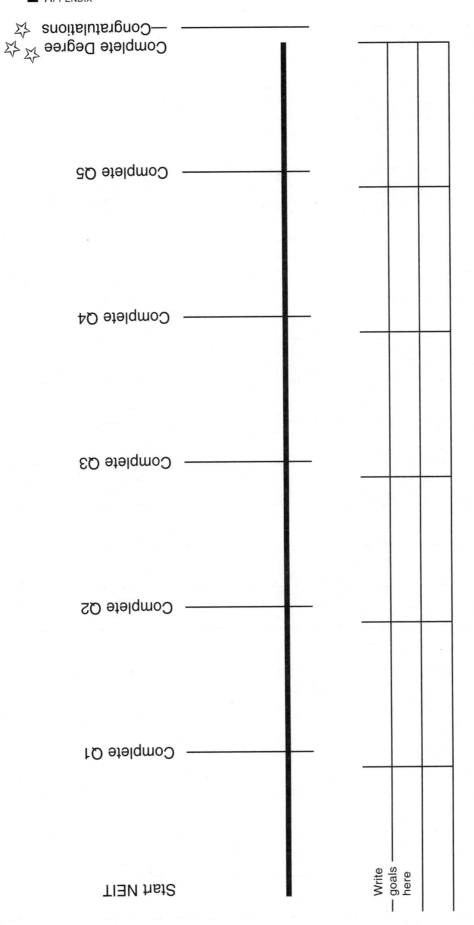

Start NEIT — Complete Q1 — Complete Q2 — Complete Q3 — Complete Q4 — Complete Q5 — Complete Degree—Congratulations ☆☆☆

Write goals here

Add as many goals as you would like to achieve within the time frame of completing your degree. This may include the goal of a particular grade point average (GPA), or the goal of perfect attendance each quarter.

Check off each goal as it is completed. Each check mark will put you closer to the ultimate goal of completing your degree.

■ Activity 5-1. Computer Skills Assessment Chart

In the first column, list the skills that you have identified as necessary for Quarter One. In the second column, rate your current level of skill on a scale of 1 to 5 (1 = no skill, 2 = little skill, 3 = moderate skill, 4 = good skill level, 5 = expert level skill). In the third column, identify the strategy that you will use to improve your skill level.

Skill	Current Level of This Skill	Strategy to Improve This Skill

■ Guidelines for Self-Assessment

As you know, the last item for your Career Inventory Folder is a self-assessment of what you have learned this quarter in TEC 101. This is your opportunity to critically and thoroughly reflect on your learning experiences and tell your facilitator what grade you think you deserve in the course.

To help you in this endeavor, the major goals of TEC 101 are listed below:

- To provide students with an orientation to NEIT and the support services that are available to them.
- To provide students with an opportunity to evaluate their computer competencies and to learn how to use technology to access information.
- To encourage students to explore their career choices and the opportunities it provides.
- To encourage students to take responsibility for their own learning and develop personal management skills.

Use these goals as a guideline to write a reflective paper in which you cite specific examples of the progress you have made in achieving these goals. For example, the first goal listed is to provide an orientation to NEIT. Ask yourself specifically, "What did you learn about the history and mission of NEIT?" For the third goal, "What did you learn about your technical career choice (skills required, career opportunities) from the materials that you downloaded from the Internet and/or the interviews that you conducted?" Once you have specifically identified what you have learned, ask yourself how this information will help you to plan for the future. You may continue in this fashion using the goals to help you focus on what you learned in each module.

Finally, based on what you have just written and your attendance at class, tell your facilitator what grade you honestly think you deserve.

Remember that the paper is a professional presentation: it should be neatly typed and free from grammatical and mechanical errors.

■ Activity 9-2. Documentation of Performance of Community Project

Community Enrichment/TEC 102
Karen Arnold, Director
Feinstein Enriching America Program

Student Name: _____ ID #: _____

Community Site/Project: _____

Supervisor: _____ Tel. #: _____

Signature of Supervisor: _____

Date(s) of Service: _____   Number of Hours: _____

_____   _____

_____   _____

_____   _____

_____   _____

_____   _____

_____   _____

_____   _____

Describe Activities Performed at This Site/Project: _____

_____

_____

_____

■ Activity 9-3. Journal

Feinstein Enriching America Program
Karen Arnold, Director
401/ 739-5000, Ext. 3322
Office: CT 331

(Three Paragraphs)

1. **Just the FACTS** of the project/activity site:
   —Describe the organization and its role in the community.
   —Describe your functions or role within this project/activity.
   —How many hours did you volunteer? Between what dates?

2. **How did YOU benefit from this experience?**
   —**What did you learn** (about yourself, the community, others) by doing this project/activity?

3. **How did the COMMUNITY benefit from your involvement?**
   —Describe your **impact** on the community, organization, or individual.

■ Works Cited

The following sources were consulted to design the TEC 101 course and to write this text.

Armstrong, T. (1999). *7 kinds of smart: Identifying and developing your multiple intelligences.* New York: Plume.

Belote, G. A. & Lunsford, L. (1996). *The freshman year: making the most of college.* Dubuque, IA: Kendall/Hunt Publishing Company.

Berkman, R. (2000, January 21). Searching for the right search engine. *Chronicle of Higher Education,* p. B6.

Burnett, H., Gousse, K., & Stein, A. B. (1999, Spring). *The unofficial pocket guide to mechanical engineering at Tufts.* [WWW Document]. URL http://www.ase.tufts.edu/mechanical/pocketguide/

Cambridge Educational. (1999). Multimedia study skills (Version 2.0) [Computer software]. Charleston, WV: Cambridge Research Group.

Career Center. Ball State University. (23 December 1998). *Professional employment portfolios.* [WWW Document]. URL http://www.bsu.edu/careers/foliojsb.html

Carter, C. (1996). *Keys to success: how to achieve your goals.* Upper Saddle River, NJ: Prentice Hall.

Chaffee, J. (1999). *Facilitator's manual with test bank for The thinker's guide to college success* (2nd ed.). Boston: Houghton Mifflin.

Chaffee, J. (1999). *The thinker's guide to college success.* (2nd ed.). Boston: Houghton Mifflin.

Chamberlain, E. (2000, March 16). *Bare bones 101: A basic tutorial on searching the web* [WWW Document]. URL http://www.sc.edu/beaufort/Library/bones.html

College prep 101: helping students prepare for college [WWW Document]. (2000, April 6). URL http://collegeprep.okstate.edu/

Connick, G. P. (Ed.). (1999). *The distance learner's guide.* (Western Cooperative for Education Telecommunications). Upper Saddle River, NJ: Prentice Hall.

Corey, G. & Corey, M. S. (1990). *I never knew I had a choice* (4th ed.). Pacific Grove, CA: Brooks/Cole Publishing Company.

Cross, K. P. (1998). *From AAHE's 1998 National Conference on Higher Education: "What do we know about students' learning and how do we know it?"* URL http://www.aahe.org/nche/cross_lecture.htm

Downing, S. (1999). *Facilitator's manual for On course: strategies for creating success in college and in life* (2nd ed.). Boston: Houghton Mifflin.

Downing, S. (1999). *On course: strategies for creating success in college and in life* (2nd ed.). Boston: Houghton Mifflin.

Ellis, D. (2000). *Becoming a master student* (9th ed.). Boston: Houghton Mifflin.

Gardner, H. (1985). *Frames of mind: the theory of multiple intelligences.* New York: BasicBooks.

Gardner, H. (1993). *Multiple intelligences: the theory in practice: a reader.* New York: BasicBooks.

Glossbrenner, A. & Glossbrenner, E. (1998). *Search engines for the World Wide Web.* Berkeley, CA: Peachpit Press.

Hellyer, R., Robinson, C. & Sherwood, P. (1998). *Study skills for learning power.* Boston: Houghton Mifflin.

Jenkins, M. C., Kiser, J. D. & Kiser, T. R. (2000). *A basic job & career handbook: how to get a job, keep a job and change jobs.* Dubuque, IA: Kendall/Hunt Publishing Company.

Kirk, E. E. (1999, June 22). *Evaluating information found on the Internet* [WWW Document]. URL http://milton.mse.jhu.edu:8001/Research/education/net.html

Leu, Jr., D. J. & Leu, D. D. (1999). *Teaching with the Internet: lessons from the classroom.* Norwood, MA: Christopher Gordon Publishers.

Maze, S., Moxley, D. & Smith, D. J. (1997). *Authoritative guide to web search engines.* New York: Neal-Schuman.

Mencke, R. & Hartman, S. (1999). *Spring 1999 tutor training manual.* Tucson, AZ: University Learning Center, University of Arizona.

Mind Tools, Inc. *Goal setting* [WWW Document]. URL http://www.mindtools.com/pggoalst.htm

National Dropout Prevention Center. (1995). *Assessing my multiple intelligences.* Clemson, SC: Clemson University.

Osher, B. & Ward, J. (1998). *Learning for the 21st century* (5th ed.). Dubuque, IA: Kendall/Hunt Publishing Company.

Pejsa, J. (1998). *Success in college using the Internet.* Boston: Houghton Mifflin Company.

Pond, R. J. (1999). *Introduction to engineering technology* (4th ed.). Englewood Cliffs, NJ: Prentice Hall.

Ruggiero, V. R. (1999). *Becoming a critical thinker* (3rd ed.). Boston: Houghton Mifflin.

Shirley, L. (1998). *Pocket guide to multiple intelligences.* Clemson, SC: National Dropout Prevention Center, Clemson University.

Siebert, A. & Gilpin, B. (1996). *The adult student's guide to survival & success* (3rd ed.). Portland, OR: Practical Psychology Press.

Straughn, G. (1996). *Success through goal setting: be a winner, not a whiner.* [WWW Document]. URL http://www.smartbiz.com/sbs/arts/exe92.htm

Strommer, D. (Ed.). (1998). *Your college experience: strategies for success.* Belmont, CA: Wadsworth.

INDEX